A TINY SPACE
TO MOVE AND BREATHE

(notes from the fall, 1997)

Walter Holland

MOLE-BANKS TEXTWARES

© 2009 — 2012 Walter G. Holland
All rights reserved.

Mole-Banks Textwares, Cambridge, MA.

Portions of this book first appeared on *blog.waxbanks.net* and *phish.net*. Bits have been pilfered from other works by the author, which you can get wherever you got this one.

Please support your local small presses and independent bookstores.

Formatted by the author in LaTeX.

CREATESPACE EDITION OCTOBER 2012

Contents

intro   v
   nomenclature v
   basics v
   getting to 97 vii
   that was the year that was: 1997 x

now then   1
   november 13, las vegas 1
   november 14, salt lake city 10

road   21

and furthermore   29
   november 16, denver 29
   november 17, denver 38

honey, come to a phish show   45

and furthermore   49
   november 19, champaign 49
   november 21 and 22, hampton 62

inside outside   73

and furthermore   85
   november 21 and 22, hampton: redux 85
   november 23, winston-salem 91
   (let's let the master handle this next bit) 100
   november 26, hartford 101

november 28–30, worcester 106	
old break	**121**
and then sum	**141**
and furthermore	**143**
december 2 and 3, philly 143	
december 5, cleveland 156	
clearing	**159**
and furthermore	**165**
december 6, auburn hills 165	
december 7, dayton 182	
december 9, penn state 183	
december 11, rochester 183	
december 12 and 13, albany 183	
sense of an ending	**185**
we deflate	**203**
acknowledgements 203	
apologies and recommendations 203	
end of session 204	

intro

NOMENCLATURE

I've capitalized but not quoted the titles of songs, and made an effort to eliminate any ambiguity which might result from this nomenclature.

BASICS

The four-piece guitar/piano rock band PHISH formed in Vermont in 1983. In the late 90s they were by some standards the most successful touring act in the US – drawing 80,000 people to the northernmost tip of Maine for a weekend-long festival at which they were the only performers, that kind of thing. They've never had a radio hit.

Their repertoire includes hundreds of original songs, some conventional singer-songwriter stuff but with several albums' worth of multipart 'prog-rock' compositions by guitarist Trey Anastasio. Their music has always integrated tightly written ensemble work and freewheeling collective improvisations ('jams'), which eschew the standard solo/accompaniment model of rock in favour of mutable structures and coherent movement as a single entity.

The band's reputation built steadily throughout the 90s as fans traded cassettes, DATs, and later CDs of their famous live shows, which generally run three hours long across two sets. The standard concert form aids the music's function, and echoes the approach taken by the Grateful Dead, one of Anastasio's major inspirations: a first set full of shorter songs and relatively controlled improv, and a fluid second set whose improvisations often leave their song-forms and coalesce into spontaneous compositions.

The radical democracy of Phish's performances blends productively with their longtime reliance on Anastasio for songs and creative direction; in a sense it's his band, or was for a long time, and he's the focus of fan attention, just as Jerry Garcia was 'first among equals' in the eyes of Deadheads. Indeed, there's even a 'fifth member' of the band: lighting designer Chris Kuroda, whose improvised light show is essential to their live show.

They're not a jazz band, though they've drawn harmonic and energetic lessons from jazz. They do play arena rock reminiscent of bombastic Seventies acts (from Zeppelin to Floyd to Yes), but Trey Anastasio's key inspiration is probably the jazz-rock iconoclast Frank Zappa – especially his ensemble leadership, compositional aesthetic, and architectural approach to soloing. (Not to mention the dumb jokes.) Anastasio's a musical omnivore and Phish's catalogue reflects that. Those who attend a Phish concert are likely to hear several of the following: bluegrass, math-rock, straight-ahead jazz, calypso, comic rock opera, heavy metal, a fugue, some barbershop, and several varieties of funk (from James Brown snap to sly Meters shuffle to something like Miles Davis's aggressive mid–70s funk-rock).

All four players are standouts on their instruments. Anastasio is an expressive, fluent soloist, and shows incredible dexterity when moving between rhythm and lead guitar roles. Jon Fishman is among the most intuitive, flexible, and precise drummers in rock; he's arguably the most accomplished member of the band on his instrument. Keyboardist Page McConnell has the weakest chops, for what that's worth, but he's an extraordinary listener with a unique style that provides enormous amounts of harmonic material for the other two melodic players. Bassist Mike Gordon transformed in the mid–90s from a bizarro ensemble player to a gifted groove dude, and in the last four years Gordon has revealed himself as an astonishingly inventive second lead player and bandleader. The band can go from nimble pseudoclassical maneuvers to etheral ambient soundscapes to a deep rhythmic pocket in the matter of a few seconds – indeed, their signature composition You Enjoy Myself requires that they do just this, with a four-minute vocal jam to top it all off.

In October 2000, unsure where to go next after the climactic show of their early career (a midnight-to-sunrise set in the Everglades on 1/1/00), they went on hiatus for two years. On NYE 2002 they reunited, with mixed results. Trey Anastasio's drug addictions and the burden of paying the salaries of nearly their entire circle of friends took their toll, and after celebrating their 20th anniversary in late 2003 they broke up 'for good' at the Coventry festival in mid-August 2004.

Phish reunited, healthy and strong and ready to be grownups, in March 2009. Their Summer 2012 tour was unbelievable.

I've seen Phish roughly 30 times: my first show was 12/7/95 in Niagara Falls.

GETTING TO 97

On New Year's Eve 1995 at Madison Square Garden, Phish played a three-set show that was really the climax and capstone to their first decade-plus as a band. Hot on the heels of a hectic Fall Tour – 54 shows in less than three months, including a one-time Halloween cover of The Who's *Quadrophenia* in its entirety! – the band marshaled all their musical resources to showcase every aspect of their development. The first set alone included four tunes from Trey's rock opera *The Man Who Stepped Into Yesterday*,[1] a satirical cover of Collective Soul's abysmal pop hit Shine, soaring versions of their long long prog tunes Reba and The Squirming Coil, and a killer take on Maze (one of Trey's darker tunes, and a grand showoff piece for Trey and Page).

The second set, meanwhile, focused on big jams: the Who's tune Drowned opened out into a delicate instrumental interlude that smoothly segued into The Lizards (more Gamehendge), Runaway Jim took flight, and the reliable jam vehicle Mike's Song closed the set with Trey alone onstage, sculpting an eerie delay loop jam.

After some amateur setbreak theatrics, they busted into Auld Lang Syne as the clock struck midnight, then let loose a 20+ minute Weekapaug > Sea and Sand (the bracket denotes a *segue*,[2]

---

[1] Also known as 'Gamehendge,' *TMWSIY* is an impressive achievement: for his undergraduate thesis project Trey wrote an hourlong musical about the seductiveness of power and, um, a magical artifact called the Helping Friendly Book.

[2] For many Phish fans, especially the nerdy male setlist-parser sort overrepresented in online fandom, a run of smooth, unpredictable (but retrospectively inevitable) segues is the holy grail of improvised music. 'Jammed out' versions of songs – those that burst the confines of their written form, even if they only make it as far as a one-chord funk vamp – are universally prized by tape/mp3 collectors. This distorts fans' experience. The common trajectory: you like song XYZ so you seek out multiple recordings of it, but there's only so much variation between 'normal' versions, so you start to prize 'unusual' versions irrespective of their specific natures – fetishizing difference itself – and when you do go to shows your fun is (perhaps just subtly) coloured by the implication that if different==good then 'conventional' performances must needs be less good. We might undiplomatically speculate that the main reason Phish fans obsess about these form-breaking 'Type II' jams (the nomenclature isn't important) is that most human beings can't hear, or don't care about, subtler differences between versions…

an improvised bridge between songs) with Page belting out the night's second *Quadrophenia* tune over melancholy solo piano. Only *then* did they unleash a monstrous You Enjoy Myself – imagine firing up your fiendishly complicated signature tune at 1am after three or four hours of expertly-performed holiday debauchery! And to close, why not whip out Edgar Winters's glam/camp/prog/wank classic, Frankenstein?

It was a tour de force and everyone in the room knew it, not least the band. In late 1995 they'd achieved a confident, fully-formed musical identity: arena-rock grandeur, experimental psychedelia, postpunk aggression, Broadway sentiment, all in an operatic *maximalist* vein. Even their barbershop tunes were huge. (Did they in those days feature a barbershop arrangement of Skynyrd's insufferable Freebird? Yes they did. Was it funny? Yes. Once.) They'd inherited a portion of the Grateful Dead's fanbase (for better and mostly worse) and stepped up to the challenge of uniting the Dead's shaggy Bay Area lazydelia with frenetic East Coast experimentalism – like a three-way mix of Genesis, Jefferson Airplane, and Sun Ra.

The sky was the limit.

So naturally they took a big step back.

Phish spent 1996 adapting to bigger rooms and bigger expectations. They got banned from Red Rocks and threw a party in Vegas. They brought a gospel choir onstage in Boston to do Bohemian Rhapsody – aced it – and released their best studio album, *Billy Breathes*, a dweeb-rustic bit of bent Americana that closes with an *Abbey Road*-style suite of smoothly flowing tunes, ending with the useless beauty of guitar anthem Prince Caspian.

It was an alright year. I never, ever, ever listen to any of their 1996 shows. Not even the Clifford Ball, their first outsized summer festival, which drew 60,000 revelers to upstate New York to see a single band play. The Ball is widely acknowledged as a peak achievement for the band, both musically and culturally. I can't work up enthusiasm for it. It's just Good Phish, and I am not strong enough for that.

But one very important thing happened that year.

On Halloween, they played Talking Heads' afropocalypse nerdfreak party classic, *Remain in Light* – a near-perfect album, the album that contains one of the greatest, nerviest pop songs of the 80s, Once in a Lifetime – and all at once discovered the joys of minimalist dance music. The rest of the year was perfectly fine but that's the moment, right there. This is important: in 1994 they covered *The Beatles* (the 'White Album') and learned about jukebox madness; in '95 they did *Quadrophenia* and grew as large and loud as a band could grow; and in '96, not knowing what the hell to do with themselves, they began to *dance*.

THAT WAS THE YEAR THAT WAS: 1997

They played a strong batch of club shows in Europe in February and March, fleet and detailed and full of energy but only occasionally hinting at the transformation to come. Compelling variation on old themes. After several months of songwriting and rehearsal in Vermont, they returned to Europe for a few more weeks in June and July with fire in their bellies and more than a dozen new songs ready for the stage.

The Summer Europe tour alternated raucous festival crowds with tiny attentive club audiences. Stateside fans pored over Euro setlists with deepening horror, realizing some of their most cherished songs had vanished from the repertoire: Mike's Groove, You Enjoy Myself, Suzy Greenberg, Tweezer. Stories of 10- and 20-minute funk instrumentals circulated. The July 1 show had a five-song second set; July 2 they only played three tunes in the second frame (then a half-hour double encore).

Reviews were mixed and immoderate. They'd lost their minds. They were playing better than anyone had ever heard. They *weren't using setlists*. They'd forgotten who they were. It was 1977 all over again. It was all too much. Something new was coming.

Of course, Phish had always kept on becoming new. That was the *point*.

July 21 they kicked off the second half of the touring year – two coast-to-coast American tours – with a show in Virginia Beach. The opening tune: a 16-minute rendition of the porno-funk jam Ghost, a skeletal composition and minimalist polyrhythmic groovebeast built to move. By the time the curtain came down on that jam they'd effectively signaled to their many fans that they were a new band playing in a new style, ready to do something they'd never even contemplated during their first decade and a half: **less**.

The next month was a blur of increasingly tight funk playing – 'cow funk' some genius called it – and unprecedentedly *patient* group improvisation. With no setlist and plenty of time to let jams unfold on their own, the band played startlingly relaxed music with none of the twitchy comic energy or math-nerd fussiness of their previous material. Cities was back in the rotation after nearly a decade, but it rolled out slow and dirty, nothing like the zippy Talking Heads original. Ghost had filled Tweezer's rock-groove role in July, but now Tweezer was back thick as maple syrup, trading its wolf-at-the-door menace for dancefloor slither. Locomotive psychedelic rockers Gin and Bowie were heard to morph into machinic lockstep polyrhythm exercises.

It wasn't all danceadelia, of course. Trey Anastasio's new tunes put the same Talking Heads-derived minimalist toolkit to use in a variety of stylistic settings, from the lilting folk melancholy of Dirt and the carib prog waltz of Limb by Limb to Twist's eerie oscillations and Piper's frenzied gallop. The new tunes eschewed the multipart long-form structure Trey had long employed (from mid–80s staples like YEM and Fluffhead through 1994's Guyute), favouring compact intricate assemblies and rich, fluid, generative improvisatory forms.

But the big news was the funk. Like the post-'retirement' Grateful Dead, after devoting years to a singular blend of inaccessible psychedelia and sing-songy Americana, Phish stepped off in July 1997 ready to be the world's foremost (perhaps sole) hippie dance band.

After peaking again at the Great Went festival in mid-August – alternating towering, unbelievably *coherent* long-form improvisations and skittering hyperkinetic dance grooves seemingly without effort – Phish retreated into the studio and practice room for a few months. Summer's glow faded through autumn's red yellow orange brown into the early sunsets and evening chill of November.

So now here we were. Phish were a groovy dance band, it seemed: still the goofiest rock band on earth, still like a weird postpunk nerd knockoff of the Dead, but now they had some James Brown grooves and knew what to do with them.

So that was how it was gonna be.

More of that. More fun, more funk. Nothing more.

now then

I heartily recommend…*VALIS*, *The Last Testament* and *The Sirian Experiments*…to readers of this book. Unless you are locked into a very dogmatic reality-tunnel, you will have a few weird moments of wondering if Sirians *are* experimenting on us, and a few weird moments can be a liberating experience for those who aren't scared to death by them.

What is more important than such extra-mundane speculation, I think, are practical and pragmatic questions about what one *does* with the results of brain change experience…

There is a great deal of lyrical Utopianism in this book. I do not apologize for that, and do not regret it. The decade that has passed since the first edition has not altered my basic commitment to the game-rule that holds that an optimistic mind-set finds dozens of possible solutions for every problem that the pessimist regards as incurable. (Robert Anton Wilson, *Cosmic Trigger*)

NOVEMBER 13, LAS VEGAS

I: Chalkdust, BEK, Theme, Train Song, Melt, Beauty of My Dreams, My Soul, YEM, Char0 **II:** Stash, PYITE, Caspian, Bouncing, Mike's > Hydrogen > Weekapaug **E:** Loving Cup

I once argued briefly with two friends about whether Phish (my choice) or the Grateful Dead (theirs) had a deeper command of 'Black music,' which I eventually realized is an offensive way of framing the question. (For comparison: what would it mean to have a command of 'White music,' anyhow?) What I meant was that Phish had absorbed the sound of Black dance music of the 70s–90s – the intersection of soul, jazz, R&B, funk, and (later on) hip-hop that produced the template for nearly all popular (i.e. *teenagers'*) music today – while the Dead could never handle the lockstep minimalism of funk and its descendants.

The counterargument, simply put, was that Phish had little or no connection to Black music of the *early* 20th century – the complexly integrated popular roots of bluegrass, folk, and indeed jazz – and Dead tunes like 'He's Gone' (with its incantatory *a cappella* outro: 'Oooh, nothing's gonna bring him back') got a lot closer to the Black church, say, than Phish ever could.

Well, such rankings aren't too useful. But I'm reminded of them when listening to this debut performance of Black-Eyed Katy, Phish's summary memorandum re: their midyear experiments in New Orleans jazz/funk beatmaking. There's nothing to the tune but one silly, rickety bass riff, and of course the effortless modulation into that slinky back-barroom jam, which for a single tour was Trey's premier guitar showcase. During their time off in early 1997 the band had honed their funk chops by playing along with Meters records, trying (largely in vain) to match that seminal New Orleans band's coldfire rhythmic restraint. It was a literal patience exercise: the quartet would play along with the beginning of a track, mute the record while still playing their own groove, and then join in at the end, invariably to find that they'd unconsciously sped up while the Funky Meters had maintained their smoothass tempo.

BEK sounds like one of those exercises falling joyfully apart. This is the weakest version of Black-Eyed Katy they played

– hesitant, anticlimactic, the arrangement not yet figured out. Interestingly (but unsurprisingly), the Vegas BEK jam sounds more like Phish's other music than any other version: the climactic crescendo hints at spacey psych-rock textures which would be pared away in later performances. Still, there's an intrinsic power to that loping midtempo groove. You might say they'd taken a specific kind of Tweezer jam and given it a little swagger, a specifically *static* quality. The song's in no danger of going anywhere unusual, so there's no need to apologize for its self indulgence.

That tendency to tacitly apologize in performance is (I'd argue) a big part of Phish's musical identity. Or it used to be. The humour in their music isn't *just* a gleeful yes to Frank Zappa's famous question – it's a kind of compensation for the music's occasional inaccessability, a peace offering. After 1995 or 1996 Phish just stopped saying sorry, though. Crucially, they also (mostly) stopped being so funny. The happiness in Phish's Fall 97 shows isn't anymore manic electric foolishness; it's actual joy, streaked with relief.

At having survived the cold, I mean.

The Vegas version of Theme from the Bottom isn't unusual, but it differs in one crucial respect from earlier performances: like everything else Phish played in late 1997, it sounds like the band have all day to play, and know it, and are in no great hurry to fill the time.

It's impossible to overstate how important that specific feeling – literal timelessness – is to the music and *culture* of Phish.

Could you listen to one track at the same *tempo,* in the same overall mood, for say thirty minutes? Listening to *Endtroduc-*

ing... this morning I was wondering what an entire album that sounded like 'Midnight in a Perfect World' would feel like. Only it's not the same tempo I mean, exactly. The same feeling. Pervasive melancholy and longing. Dissolution at night's end. Now that I'm a father and turn in early at night, I cherish that feeling – more than I ever did when I was actually experiencing it so many nights. When you look up from a conversation you settled for (she did too) and realize the room has emptied out and now you have to follow, to be Late again. Again to insert yourself into someone else's circumstance. Or just lying in bed next to someone too tired to do anything at all except to float or flow along some invisible line of current, shared. Become the same sea. (I mean that time is the movement and I mean that love is the sea. Or I'm getting carried away.)

Anyway I was wondering that. Phish's music doesn't quite have that quality; certainly not now if ever it did. But they've come close so many times. The dark at the edge of sound. Already so deep and it's growing always. Fall 97 has that feel for me, like it's all one song. One exhalation.

The weird thing about *Endtroducing...* (in these terms only; it's not a weird nor Weird album) (though there are monsters inside and ghosts) is that what I experience as an all-enveloping single emotion is channeled through a variety of tempos and moods and genres. 'Building Steam,' 'Stem/Long Stem,' and 'Mutual Slump' are gothic horror, the latter two shot through with an unexpected machine violence; 'Organ Donor' notquite fits the same mold; 'Scatter Brain' and 'Number Song' take the tempo way up; 'Napalm Brain' may as well be one of Trey's Hendrix-inspired wah-death breaks. What I think of as the paradigmatic *Endtroducing...* mood is embodied by a handful of tracks: 'Changeling,' both parts of 'What Does Your Soul

Look Like,' 'Midnight' of course, and the three 'Transmission' interludes.

I've long had it in my head that the album is full of this latenight wiped out melancholy, and that it's *sexy* – is it? – but the sexiness isn't quite to do with sex; or it's precisely the fact that the promise is unfulfilled that makes it a promise (which is beautiful) and not a fact (which merely perfectly *is*). Compare to, say, *Let's Get It On*, which *is itself sex* in musical form, but which doesn't hold the same erotic charge for me.

Which is to say that my wife is right: *Endtroducing...* isn't a bedroom album. Sorry love.

(You could make a perfect bedroom mix taking individual tracks from John Zorn's Masada albums. The pent-up midtempo stuff.)

I bring all this up only to make the linked points that, OK, what's sexy is very much a function of who and where you are right now, yes yes, but also (much more pertinent to a too-long thing about Phish in Fall 97) I'm betting everyone finds that one long track at one tempo is *a sexual rather than an erotic ideal* – it's the old male fantasy of *more* imposed on a medium of just *now*. I have a dollar, I would prefer two dollars. You're fucking one person, two must be better. We hear five minutes of blissful ambient music, thirty minutes must obviously be preferable.

So much of Phish fandom really is just a Committee of More. It makes sense: the music generates that desire, even as its inevitable movement ('disappointment') spares us from the ego-fright of finding out that, surprise, too much of a good thing is usually boring.

Phish gets dinged all the time for 'interminable two-chord jams' or whatever. But here's how you know they're masters: they know when to go deep and they know when to come up for air. Phish's music lacks the monotonic *sexual* quality of (say) the Disco Biscuits – a post-Phish 'jamtronica' band given to setlong techno jams short on risk and wit and long on…well, just *long* – but makes up for it with a heady erotic always-presence. On their best nights they get to a place of total unification and continuity through an unbelievable *variety* of mechanism: a weirdly placed calypso beat here, wail of major-chord guitar there, wisely to end this addictive funk groove now, time (I mean space!) opening up ahead.

All at once a pileup of detail and a free flow forward.

None of which is really present in the Vegas Black-Eyed Katy, which after it all is just a competent funk-up-a-tiny-hill guitar jam. But it'll make more sense later.

When it went down (well before the era of next-day mp3s online), Black-Eyed Katy, Mike's Groove, and Stash were the news – but the reports on this Stash were mixed and muddled. The usual suspects did their usual 'wonderful but nowhere near as good as 7/2/97' thing, and everyone seemed to agree that this Stash was interesting but…weird. 'It lost me in places,' one reviewer told the Phish newsgroup.[3]

It was the future, of course. Out of turn.

Listening now you can hear the outlines of the band's later experiments in ambient sound. Page goes nuts on piano start-

---

[3] *rec.music.phish*, for a long time the center of online Phish fandom and now a ghost town like 99% of Usenet. Like a discussion forum independent of the Web, pure text like email, so it worked as a kind of glorified mailing list off in its own parallel computational universe. Usenet was fantastic – the center of the Internet, for a while. Once spam arrived it was over, of course. Spam and sociopathy ruin every digital communications forum if left unchecked.

ing roughly eight minutes into the tune, leading with dissonant fistfuls while the rest of the band motors along. Trey cools his own busy line out, folding in to a single insistent note after a moment, then starts in with a jagged minor-chord sway, like the theatre manager clearing his throat before announcing that the Soviets have won the space race. While the 'rhythm section' (what a limited term for what Mike and Fish do) thrashes underneath, Trey then does something unexpected and right: he streeeeetches into his upper register just after the ten minute mark to suggest a sonic alternative, giving the music a little space rather than squeezing the whole band's sound into such a narrow frequency range.

Page responds with eerie analog synth chords and the clouds thin. Stars beyond. Trey begins to alternate between the sinister minor-key Stash jam and its twinkling relative major, but before we can go sublime the whole band makes a turn toward a ghostly ambient space. Descending whole tones from Trey, not so off you can't hold on, and sweet electric piano from Page, while Mike switches from a moving image to static sonics, and Fishman strips down to a hushed cymbal jog punctuated by rimshots and those high-frequency tom toms he favoured back then.

After fourteenish minutes we're floating in space. Four minutes later the hull begins to heat up and we reenter the atmosphere as screams become again audible. Some monster is killing the crew. Maybe it's the piano player. 'Maybe so, maybe not.' Done by 22:00.

♥ ☞ ❀ ☞ ✻

I (used to) play the sax so naturally in college I'd stay up into the wee hours jamming with friends. I can tell you this: it's not hard to get into outer musical space. In fact you can *start* there if you like. Does it 'count' if you do? That makes no sense. All that matters is that you listen, honour silence, give your sound, don't bullshit. We could play pretty music, and rock at times. Once I even got on the piano and we jammed on 'Frankie Sez' though I didn't tell anyone that's what I was playing.

But anyway we couldn't – *no one could* – do what Phish did in those days. Stash is a complicated tune with very stupid lyrics and an unforgettable guitar melody that modulates like a zillion times during a maddening dissonant instrumental interlude before the final chorus – 'Is it for this my life I sought? Maybe so, maybe not.'[4] The four-cornered jam that winds its way out of the song is very much an extension of the tune itself, with a tight structure and a strong trajectory toward a clearly-defined goal. Like its brother tune David Bowie, nearly every version of Stash rides a modal swerve up a long crescendo before that on-a-dime unison statement to close. The bandmembers' oft-stated ideal of being 'part of one big chord,' moving with the internal fluidity and extraordinary cohesion of a flock of birds, really shines through on tunes like Stash, which afford the players both modal freedom and chordal solidity.

But the Vegas Stash is something else again: for a second the band leaves the gravitational pull of the Stash structure (i-VIb-iidim7-V7b9 I think) and just *floats*, without ever losing sight of their home planet. Remember when Trinity and Neo break through the clouds in the third *Matrix* movie[5] and just

---

[4]See what I mean about stupid lyrics? That approaches *Fifty Shades of Grey*-level clumsiness.

[5]I might be the only person alive who thinks *The Matrix* is made infinitely richer by its sequels, which completely undo its nerdpunk heroics; but then I though the end of *Avatar* was a transhumanist psychedelic nightmare and one of the scariest things anyone had ever put up on an American movie screen. No one takes the really crazy ideas seriously, though. I've written about all this before: *http://blog.waxbanks.net/2011/02/if-i-had-a-chance-to-interview-*

hang there in the sunlight for a second, and you know they'll fall again so the moment is cracked glass and already breaking as it's born, but pure – pure joy, pure love? This is that moment, for four minutes. It's not 'pretty' or a relief in the sense that five seconds of bright sunlight out of eight twilit hours of *Matrix* movies are a relief; it's just a pure moment.

And it can't exist without the tight structure. It isn't *just* floating, you couldn't have started out there; it's *release*. A sense of impending doom doesn't just precede these moments of what video gamers call 'extra life,' it creates them.

So many Phish tunes are preoccupied with water: surrendering to the flow, splitting and melting, splashing in the sea. This music begins as *ice* and freezes again as the lights come up. Meanwhile it becomes where we were once born and may yet be.

Of course this isn't even the 'best' Stash for my money. That's Amsterdam, 7/2/97 – what a year for that tune! – which over a half-hour follows a parallel path through different elevations to one of the great musical vistas in Phish's whole concert history. But isn't that kind of comparison a little bit…daft? The Amsterdam Stash reached a restful sunlit spot, but the eerie freeze of the Vegas Stash is its own private triumph, its own name – and it's the only musical journey that could ever produce that musical experience. Does that make sense?

Ranking/rating is a social power game. End transmission.

---

keanu-reeves.html.

NOVEMBER 14, SALT LAKE CITY

I: Jim, Gumbo > Maze > FEFY, 2001 > Funky Bitch, Guyute, Antelope **II:** Wolfman's Brother > Piper > Twist > Slave **E:** Bold As Love

When I first got into Phish there were no official live releases; it wasn't until *A Live One*, Phish's first gold record (if memory serves) and a fine document of how they were playing in 1994, that I heard a couple of the band's unreleased staples (Hood, Gumbo, Slave). It was the *Live One* version of Harry Hood that turned me into a true believer – I spent most of Summer 1995 listening to the album over and over, that track especially. I'll never forget coming home from my super-nerdy residential pre-college program at Fine East Coast Liberal Arts School, hanging out at a friend's house, and making everyone lie down on the floor in the dark and listen closely to that one 15-minute song.

None of them were as excited as I was.

The big difference between Phish fandom then and now was that mp3 audio wasn't around to make digital Phish collections feasible. It was all analog cassettes – Maxell XL-II purchased in bulk, thank you very much – and Phish fans of any level of 'seriousness' were bound to have dozens or even hundreds of the damn things taking up their valuable shelf space. You had to reach out to other fans to get tapes; the music had physical form, it was an object which could come under your control or be horrifyingly *lost* – or found. I lived out in the country back then, and the music on the tapes was like a shortwave transmission from another world. Like the weird sounds of the *Conet Project*: electromagnetic memorial whispers, modern mystery cults. Maybe another whole country hidden inside mine, or me.

Runaway Jim and Gumbo led off the show following the Vegas bash in November. As it happens I'd heard great versions of both tunes at Star Lake in Summer 97 – the Star Lake Gumbo is one of the most engaging jams of the year, actually, evolving from slap-pop dance funk through guitar anthem into ambient-sparkle outro without apparent effort. It's hard to reassemble the musical content of that evening in memory, though; the purely personal overlay – innocence and unexpressed need and not knowing what was or wasn't (it wasn't) 'true love' – is impossible to see through, and whatever I might remember I can only reencounter now through the medium of the recording.

Which isn't anything like being there. That's more like walking through a forest and hearing the earth whisper that once there was an ocean here and to see the fish from below they seemed to be flying. Or something. No it's not actually like that.

I did love her of course and she loved me but 'love' is too big a word for too complex a thing and I was too small a person. Maybe you know all this your own way.

This is a decent Runaway Jim but 'nothing special' as the tape dweebs say. Gumbo is fantastic. One of those songs that benefited enormously from what by rights should've been a lockstep lurch blind through a cluttered room, but always came out cool for some reason. No tune that loafs with such indolence into blahblahsville should be allowed to exist, but Gumbo does and it's goddamn wonderful. The 'E Center' version peters out but good; it's one of those group improvisations that has nowhere to go, does so, and then just kinda lies down on the ground and sleeps.

The fact that they follow up Gumbo with a wild version of their uptempo burner Maze is one of the sure signs that this is a great show – the instinctive move toward melodramatic martial dissonant minor-key thrash after that dance groove is a perfect choice, but one that commits the band to a dark or destructive course for the set. Gumbo's a dark blue jam right around 85bpm, after all; Maze moves like daggers but isn't exactly *sprightly*. But it keeps the mood, whatever it is, going strong – even with its dramatic change of style and tempo.

Nightfall. That's what it sounds like to me, this whole show: night falling.

Maybe it's the drugs.

No not *my* drugs.[6] The band's well-known descent into narcotic dissolution, which led to the two-year hiatus in October 2000 and their calamitous 'permanent' breakup at the Coventry festival in 2004, is said to have begun in 1996–97. Phish fandom exploded after the death of Jerry Garcia in 1995, and the theretofore familial crowds welcomed the fratboys, hangers-on, and predatory transients looking for a decent-sized drug market. The backstage scene changed too – Phish had never shied away from drugs but now psychotropics of every sort became central to the cultural experience before, during, and after the show.

'2001' – really Deodato's disco-funk arrangement of the sunrise from Strauss's *Also Sprach Zarathustra* – was a quick rhythm exercise for Phish until late 1996, when the lessons of their Halloween cover of Talking Heads' *Remain in Light* fully sank in and they began to let their dance grooves *breathe* for a damn change. The first extended versions of 2001 appear then, but the song wasn't a jam centerpiece until Summer 97, at which point its

---

[6] The nurse practitioner ordered me to suck on Sour Patch Kids in case my salivary gland was blocked, so I'm doing that. They're *disgusting*. Do people really eat these things for fun?

value as a bopping minimalist funk showcase became apparent and it started blowing up into 15–20 minute explorations of groove.[7]

In 1998–99 '2001' would take on new dimensions – the ar-rhythmic ambient intro stretching up to ten minutes and Trey's guitar work getting increasingly textural – and after the hiatus it would lose steam and reduce to a brief clattering interlude, but here in Salt Lake City (even halfway through the first set!) 2001 is the *sauce*, all midtempo swagger and arrogant polyrhythms. This is the second show since the last performance of the tune at the Great Went, and the two versions couldn't be more different, though the basic ingredients are exactly the same.

Listen (please do listen) for Trey's guitar trills at the end, over his own compressed looping chord noise. Something strange there. Hendrix? Something. Something a little out of place but perfect: can't help but make a new space for it.

♥ ☞ ✿ ☞ ✳

I reviewed this show for the phish.net a while back. Here's how that went:

> Historical note: Fall '97 was a great time for Wolfman's Brother. Though it's a standalone tune now as it was in 1999–2000, the Wolf's Bro was a 'Type II' vehicle in 1997–98, and all four Fall versions (11/14, 11/19, 11/30, 12/7) end in gin-u-wine segue arrows, and earn them. In those days the song's sly minimalist

---

[7] If you're curious, grab the rocket-launch 2001 from the Great Went in mid-August 97, which hits a groove about 18 minutes in and rides that thang to a distant planet where everyone's having better sex than you are and they want to show you pictures and the pictures are super tasteful and nicely composed but still a turn-on. Even the framing is nice! Who's *taking* these pictures?! You don't have to be ashamed about any of it though. Just park that rocket and pull up an air mattress and leave your keys in the kiddie pool, and we'll see what happens.

funk was central to the band's improvisatory approach – for the first time Phish weren't afraid to play sexy dance music and MEAN it, so their dance tunes could integrate smoothly into the overall flow of a long-form improvisatory set.

(Compare to the awkward, clattering stop/start Tweezer experiments of the early-mid 90s, say, before Phish were able to play dance-funk without placing tongue firmly in cheek; look too at the number of early YEMs that swerved off into clever quote-a-thons and ancient riffs, as opposed to their slinky late–90s style and today's dead serious rock approach.)

Now for this transcendent show…

The second set really is what it looks like: Wolfman's > Piper > Twist > Slave, offering all the ethereal delicacy and enveloping darkness of late 1997 to a tiny, attentive crowd. Wolfman's Brother clonks back and for for a while before developing a spacey echt-'97 groove, all hazy atmospherics and feathery drumbeats; as the jam opens up a welcoming major-chord pattern evolves, and Piper bubbles up in its own time. It's a lovely Piper, building slowly to a midtempo climax – the song hadn't yet turned into a musical greyhound race in those days. After the late lamented Piper coda, Trey starts up the haunting original Twist arrangement…

…and (surprise surprise) Fall '97 was a good time for Twist too. Trey keeps things mellow with his guitar comping, Mike lets some weird dissonant chords loose from his bass, Page plays some tricks on the piano, Fishman is his usual larking-gnome self behind the drumkit, and the groove involutes and complicates into a gorgeous full-band statement – a futuristic precursor to 11/22's 'space jam' out of Halley's Comet. Trey hangs out in the ionosphere, soloing for several minutes, as the other players drop out. This is the template: between this Twist jam and the ambient Stash from the previous night in Vegas you can discern the outline of the whole tour's weeks-long subterranean melody. It's a powerfully emotional moment wholly distinct from, say, Trey's digital delay loop jams from Back in the Day (e.g. 12/31/95, 5/7/94).

The opening chords of Slave coalesce out of the mist, and the next 15 minutes are sublime. It's a short set (less than an hour!), but the music flows so effortlessly that it seems like one long song. This is dream-music – musical psychedelia in the truest sense of the word.

Writing for a fan audience is a strange thing; fans' prior knowledge and deep prejudices make enormous difficulties for anyone aiming for didactic presentation. In retrospect I'm not even sure who that 'review' is for – it's too elementary for pure fanstuff but relies too much on insider knowledge to work for a general audience.

If you've ever wondered how Phish fans talk to *each other* about this kind of thing, there's one example: impressionistic reports of (as you can see) literally unspeakable experience.

Been reading Ted Gioia's loving, generous teaching-text *The Jazz Standards* and remembering that part of the reason for Phish's musical isolation is that *no one else plays their songs*. It's hard to imagine another band even *learning* tunes like You Enjoy Myself or David Bowie despite their forgiving symmetries and systematicity.[8] Even if you did, you'd still face the problem of improvising in Anastasio's complex style – not his solo guitar playing but the ensemble approach that's an essential component of those early long-form compositions.

---

[8]Bowie's two composed sections each work short repeating phrases through a series of straightforward modulations to maintain freshness, tagged each time with chromatic footraces to close; they sound complicated (and they are glorious) but there's not as much too them as a first listen might suggest. Reba and YEM are more haphazardly constructed, with more moving parts – easier for the players to pick up after getting lost but more taxing for listeners.

I don't just mean, as so many fans[9] clearly think, that 'the jamming is the whole point of the show.' That wasn't remotely true of Phish concerts until 1993ish, at which point they'd reached maturity as improvisers and could build long portions of their shows around cohesive group jams without losing momentum (or their audience). Rather, Trey's long compositions are generally oriented toward climactic improvisations – much moreso than his punchier tunes (Gumbo, Wolfmans' Brother) tend to be. The band's shared aspiration – four improvisers combining at all times into 'one big chord,' meaning a single internally-complex moving organism rather than solo/accompaniment – is fully realized during those closing jams, when several minutes' labour 'seeding' the audience's musical processors with sound pays off at entry into the relative simplicity of improvisatory space.

There's no point in walking up to the precipice of Bowie's jam segment and just stopping, because *the song isn't done yet.* Same for Slave, obviously – it's barely a song at all – and less obviously for YEM, which used to close with three distinct improvisatory passages (two-chord funk jam, bass/drums weirdness, vocal jam(!)). Reba has nowhere to go but bliss after its maddening contrapuntal 'chase' section, and tunes like Fluffhead and Trey's much derided latter-day song Time Turns Elastic really need that rock'n'roll wail to release the enormous tension built up through 15 minutes of cat-and-mouse ensemble playing. Maze is written *towards* its wild closing jam, as is Run Like an Antelope; at least Maze would *exist* if you lopped off its

---

[9] 'Jam-chasers' are overrepresented online. It makes for lots of dispiriting arguments over which live recordings are 'worth your time' as a listener – as if the audience's time on the night in question were wasted on *suboptimal improvisation*. This egotistical notion is central to Phish's fan culture. I'm guilty here.

keyboard/guitar solos, but Antelope is basically two minutes of teasing and ten minutes of unhinged E-minor nastiness.

If your band can't maintain cohesion through these tunes' collective improvisations – not just getting the chord changes right but improvising in that barreling way Phish have – you can't actually play the tunes. And the same goes for listening, in a way: Phish's music is famously welcoming and upbeat, but there's an essential challenge in listening to improvised music that's both (1) too coherent and structured to allow total listener dissociation and (2) still shooting off in four or eight or ten directions at once like a flock of math-addled nightingales.

So then Trey didn't really start writing 'portable' music, anything that could enter the shared pop language, until maybe 1995–96. Plenty of people heard songs like Sample in a Jar or (less likely but more pleasantly) Bouncin' Around the Room in the early 90s, but what kind of band would actually cover Bouncin'?[10] It's basically a machine for producing a specific, peculiar, totally enveloping rhythmic/harmonic space – achieving blissful release of the extraordinary tension built up through its tight four-cornered arrangement. Without the right instrumentation, without the right *sound* – particularly Trey's uniquely compressed singsongy guitar tone – you may as well forget it.[11]

---

[10]There are Phish tribute bands, of course, as bearable as you'd imagine; and there's the *Sharin' in the Groove* tribute album, which shows off Trey's compositional strengths, though I'll bet you ten bucks *no one* still listens to that disc.

[11]This is paradoxically true of Sand, one of the least compelling songs Trey ever wrote – barely a song at all, really just a groove with *whatever* lyrics splashed on top – which until 2010 never quite fit with Phish's sound, but which anyone could come happily steal (good riddance). It's an unsurprising fan favourite: a plodding bass riff and one chord *ad nauseam* for 10–20 minutes, which Phish fans in all their unhappy demographic homogeneity can cheerily, awkwardly dance to. ... Well now. 1999–2000 was an experimental time for the band – the apex, or arguably the nadir, of their commitment to machinic minimalism, fluid improvisation shackled to really terrible songs.

Trey stopped writing long Frankensteinlike[12] tunes for Phish (with one awkward exception) when he started focusing on more conventionally structured pop/rock tunes, however idiosyncratically and even brilliantly arranged. (He cranked out an unbelievable collection of songs in mid–1997: Twist, Limb, Farmhouse, Dirt(!), even weirdoes like Vultures and Saw It Again…) Still, he didn't quite move from writer-for-Phish to 'American songwriter' until after Coventry, with tunes like Come As Melody (for the Trey Anastasio Band), Light, Twenty Years Later, Steam, and Backwards Down the Number Line – those last two are mixes of great music and stupid/frustrating lyrics, but well-formed songs for all that.

If Phish had a lyricist on par with Robert Hunter they'd get more popular recognition, I think; Tom Marshall is clever and sometimes witty but largely ill-suited to songwriting despite Trey's valiant efforts to set Tom's words to music. Still, Trey's writerly sensibility is so peculiar, and his work as an *arranger* so specific to his ensemble, that it's hard to imagine a 'standard' ever flowing from his pen. And that's before the problem of, y'know, the *jamming*, which is what most of us show up for in the first place, and which no one else can quite do or, indeed, has ever quite done. Alas for rock music.

Ha, see what I did there: I started off boosting Robert Hunter's lyrics, then gave the Dead the backhand! Par for the course from a fucking Phish fan. Is this the place to point out that Garcia was ten times the conventional short-form songwriter Trey is, but could never *touch* Trey's skill at arranging, long-form work, or –

And it all starts here! In 1997 I mean, not *this footnote*.

[12]Frankenstein was the maker, *Adam* the monster, but you know what I mean.

the hardest to explain – Trey's remarkable mix of rhythm/lead prowess, which is his most important feature as an improviser and maybe the single essential ingredient of Phish's collective improvisatory approach.

More on that later.

This second set really is transcendent stuff. Trey's 'space jam' solo in Twist – fluttering whorls and spirals, cascades and cataracts down rounded from his upper register dissipating finally in that weird little custom guitar's hazy midrange – emerges around the eleven-minute mark, but only after two minutes of slow buildup, with martial guitar downstrokes marking off square spaces for Mike's ringing fifth-string bass work. The piano finally shatters, Fish's drums go for expanse, and Trey almost has no choice but to give in to that way *way* prolix updownward stuff. They're in the relative major of the Twist jam's usual minor *clonk*. That's not new and it's sure not 'interesting,' especially not from a math'n'drugs band, but it's amazing how smooth that transition is.

Nothing here interferes with that powerful mood. Whenever I imagine the E Center it's really dark inside, and outside: a trackless desert. I've been through Utah, I think, but never *to* it. And never seen a show there or indeed anywhere west of Star Lake. Although. But whatever. But although.

road

(excerpt from The Allworlds Catalogue)

Crisscrossing what seemed to be the whole crumbled or rebirthing world, old but newly surpriseful, two three times a year looking for a principle of pursuit; I mean to say looking for whatever it is that people are known to have looked for, across years and decades from which you've come to regret your absence over the years. But a world only in the sense of, naturally, a horizon of possibility, or of knowledge; there was a Beyond, or at least a Besides, out past blackening nightborders, but it was beyond the point. Or beneath you. It's easy enough after a while simply to point the van down the fastest-moving highway lane within easy reach and make of the hour a *movement* – give yourself over often enough to that loop's languor and in time you may lose what roots you to any present spot. (A point has no substance or place: only surrounding.)

There was a rock band.

Or hothouse jazz, deep blue southern wail, spry mountainside reeling, greasy guitar documentary; or a skinny girl in leg warmers and a knit hat recollecting the musical litany she came up under, her grandmothers' musics. Or a multiply addicted Russian from Chicago who thinks so fast on his guitar you wouldn't believe it, but in two years he'll be dead or demolished so follow fast.

And there was a chance to chuck everything and empty out what you'd begun to think of (as) yourself, and you took took took it, so here you are, as American now as civil obedience and stockbrokers and freezer-packed pie, chasing the story of a true thing which once grew deep beneath the shared skin, feeding the shared body. Didn't young people choose how they might grow old, once? Wasn't there a straight safe broad sunbleached path which a thousand generations (or at least your parents' generation) beat on down for those to come, for you, thickly overgrown now? Without any responsibilities to speak of you could unmoor yourself, kick loose what timepieces had gathered parasitic upon your body. Why the fuck not. There'd be money, presumably; or, OK, hopefully. As if the difference is so simply recognized or named, for folks like you. Us. Presumed-world entire. Jesus, you've never worried a word's worth in your life. If it's life.

So then off you go. And here you hear:

Summer sheds for downwind fried-funk open-air sloven unfurling. Alpine Valley, Star Lake, Deer Creek, Shoreline, Desert Sky, the Gorge. Small stadia and amphitheatres roiling thick air through Fall Tour and into windwhipped winter, tight wound prickpointed surgical jab and sword, spiral whirl of psychedelic noise clamber up out of Rhodes piano and bounce hard off sparking bass guitar slap sawtoothed. Names that every generation learns again, then loses – names going away, becoming only *brands*. The Mothership. The Knick. The Garden. The Centrum. The Palace.

And for Christmas look forward to New Year, tripping toward the other Garden, or no now Fleet, and but now some other goddamn bank's name but the parquet still moans as ghosts pass. Damn. Folks have *died* for this place. Ringing grand circle song at midnight counts down, a great light, *auld lang syne* spoken soundwise. Cheers to Mr Burns, beastly dead, for olden quaintly beforethought endeavour a landslide (just the sound of it, *listen*), and find yourself a city, a city to live in...

(Did I forget to mention Memphis?)

World's contours traced timely, unspaced: highway distances collapse into unweighted graph's edges, the whole country's a map of our shared imagination (*but it all works out; I'm just a little freaked out*), at 3am through brokedown van windows the country's a past light – if there's a world out there anyway it wanna peek out from underneath the mapmaker's signature, our penstrokes Woven across dark fabric of Get Get Get to the Show (reverie ends, world ends, new world borne by new light), the Show, damn baby the Show...

For a couple of years in there you hardly listen to anything else. Weirdly you're not the only one. It's surprisingly easy to give over to a purely internal logic like that; so many other things work that way without troubling to be groovy giving and game. Party politics frinstance, like Aunt Sheila's, oh my god. The whole point of getting out into the world with its distant borders waving in summer heat (or blanketed in snow that frosts prickly down unto blue ice crackling clear) was to unmake the monomyth you threatened to become, right? To unhear for a while the story that falsely insists upon Oneness. Received truth. It's so lonely. To find out if the overheard mutter and wave swish whisper (the sound, the *Show*) really was the party you always thought everyone else was having, strangers you envied even in their Strangeness, abstractly. You always wondered whether it was fun they were having, that Weird wail, the enciphered language that snuck in under slammed doors against unwelcome cold (can't hurt you) or windows keeping good families safe from bad families (can't hurt you). Difference itself. Which springs from the world-that-is-the-Self too, though back then you hadn't taken enough drugs or dwelt long enough naked abed after the gold glow of blissful gethering had faded (that smile of his or hers dissolving impurely beautiful to an evening light, peaceful utterly and yes new) to know that. But Aunt Sheila, bless her heart – what a life she's had, you know? whereas Mom got all the luck – with Sheila there's a point where no amount of teenage trauma can justify that level of histrionic brittleness and passive aggression, or frankly just aggressive passivity, see she's too Correct at the level of her ideas to need merely to be Good at the level of actually just for once coming down from her soapbox-mountain fastness and y'know heading out into the word…

(there's that world again)

…so maybe what you're atoning for isn't just being born a couple decades too late to ever believe the crazy story that the world could be known, that a tank of gas and a wild spirit or whatever could ever be enough to carry you all the way past the idea of borders or mere being to to to the threshold of revelation, where you might become air, might *sublime* – but, nah, atoning also for the monomyth, or maybe we mean the *monologue,* a world maddening small speaking with one insistent voice, void, drowning anyone else who'd brave to speak. Not just Sheila, who when you've calmed down a little you can totally see why she'd defend herself, even after the murder of her guardian selves had long since come to completion: why she'd wish to be a whole person, a closed shape or line, even if she were shadow inside; nope, the world you're after is to be purposefully and purely and ecstatically incomplete, never to worry, never to part, never to take unnecessarily or sicken into selfishness – *oh* – it's the very idea of ever being *finished* or *whole* that clutches at you, black laughter nightmerrily at exposed edges of your sleep. (So long since you soundly could sleep alone; then again, neither could you dwell too long alongside anyone, inside; will we confess…?)

And yeah every Show is different, every night it's some other city's right-angled steel bone structure (clackity jack skellington makes of the lord's house a home wheresover creep cold fingerbones catch hold, skin of earth or heart of stone, never you leave a child alone; he's an American too like you and you'll be someday a skellington too *like the rest of us*), or a campground near enough a theatre near enough a town; and they 'jam,' you're always trying to explain to your friends or whoever, twenty minutes tracing skyward a wildening helix, eight hands twined as base pairs, *perfect concord*. (God amighty you wish you could birth a noise so finely formed, is that what gifting birth feels like? Or *being born?*)

But you live in the collapsing graph edges, the higher Way, not those disembodied points. The music falls away night upon night to become beacon – huh – or to beckon, I mean, children not yet conceived of…they'll record the notes and stops and lines but your own presence won't quite make it onto the tape. 'Remember that security guard who…I was there, y'know?': but now you're not. Rather the place you dwell, untimely, I mean timeless, is that *between* where you spent much or most of your life anyhow. We can't bear to be nowhere in particular but where else ever have we been? Your Virginia isn't mine, nor the hunter's shed lent by generous friends where your slicksweet spiriting lips first found his, nor your spot alongside the stage at Limestone that later on in summer (in summer it's always late) where for days upon hours she seemed glittered golden to dance laughing toward you, eyes, mouth, hands, her *light*…

That world America is after all only you. That body.
Your body which dreams out to us.
Our body —

now then

Time pools around us, gathers strength for further descent, the current growing stronger; and we're lifted up (oh the sky grows wider where forever she lives, but tearfully lives-no-more, gets closer and closer still) but deeper the water and darker it grows, inward its pull and the skin grows cold; time is a drowning, death is a sea, and there is the Song which buries the living. You'll unmask (loving you will unmake) the melody of me. This is the world's becoming: this is the life of our time: the war in the world it wears at our words, we weary and wild, we drown to the deeps and dream of defeat; *time is death, time is our death.*

Though stillness too is to die by degrees. Right? Well, that's the litany hushfully repeated night by night in hotel rooms or un(godsake)winterproof tents hastily erected in the clear of brownian smoke from your inherited Good Old Dad's hatchback auto, resistant in meaning to mythmaking. No one rhapsodizes about a fucking hatchback. Well but there you are, waving away the last of the Economy fuel now glassed brownly and dissipating, ears still ringing to late Show's hardsteel waveforms redoubled by concrete gymnasium walls, *remember your earplugs you idiot,* and today ya defy any mythologizing impulse **Casper the friendly zeitgeist** might have, you're in the hatchback, fuck off, and if you're committed to anything (which you are, you absolutely are) it's

1. never to lapse into stillness, which is invisibility,

2. nor to look squarely into the flaming Sauron-eye of the past,

3. nor the waiting mouth of the future,

4. and plus *the Show,* the Show, gotta get to the Show...

Not a bad agenda for staving off self-sight, all things considered. Whatever car you're driving. It was van but now, a quickling few paragraphs on, it's the hatchback. Because embarrassment too is a kind of defensive posture. You hold your own actions at arm's length, alternating goofball flop-arm flouncing about (by posture alone let the Suits know you are flatly uninterested in whatever logic of forward progress they're peddling this decade) and painstaking arcane somatic spellwork: effort in concert to conjure from thinning air a time, or perhaps a graceful state, which you were forbidden by chance or unannounced choice from achieving naturally. Born too too late.

Damn! Whose fault is it you missed the Sixties the first time around?

(Not to nitpick here and don't take offense but umm maybe if you hadn't by travel of time shenanigans interrupted your own grandparents doing it up missionary style in the Caddy...?)

But no amount of involution or arms-crossing, no level of detailed setlist-archive collation or maintenance, no guilty canonicity of escape-dreaming (the wild world you long to visit is the *safety* of *away,* the – wait what was it – straight safe broad sun-bleached path beat on down just for you and me by the very souls we now are sworn to resent and to betray and, crying ourselves to sleep night by night in – what was it, wait – inherited homes, or hatchbacks, some day invariantly to *hate,* but they made it and they fled there long before you had the wit or will to be blue), can hold back the current's rise nor the dark deep's clutch and greed. The music falls away. Cities fall away. Worlds away.

Words weakly away. You. Will die. They within the music will die without it. We of words inaudibly will die.

(no Song of Passage will bear across the bonebrittling sea the nightward linger of her lips) (i'm there at limestone stamping all of us our muddy feet wailing *yes* into the bliss of dissolve and death when it comes will be only an intrusion of allwhite light into endless dark that was life of the body the body our body) (sweetsoaked do you bear upon warm skin still my love such a mark as a kiss leaves, even there, even as i)

and furthermore

NOVEMBER 16, DENVER

I: NICU > My Soul, Black-Eyed Katy, Farmhouse, Old Home Place, Billy Breathes, Cars Trucks Buses, Scent, Poor Heart, Taste, Hello My Baby **II:** Timber > Simple > Wilson > Hood > Izabella **E:** Bowie

The Denver shows were the Big Announcement (on the day, back in the day) that things were going to be, after all, different; there was a party in Vegas and that incredible Stash plus in the as-mentioned trackless wastes sixty perfect nightlit minutes to hush us (were you there? I wasn't there but I'm now with you there but too it can be can be everywhere) out. But Denver! Goddamn!

At this point there's no getting away from the sheer drugginess of it all. That looping noise underneath that Timber, from intro through the whole jam, 16 minutes of it – a pleasant perversity without obvious precedent in Phish's catalogue, though FX-laden up-ambient dronework would be the central stylistic feature of the band's music in late 1999…it's hard to make strict sense of the music sober. As a structural *method* there'd be something a little antagonistic about 16-minute dissolute swell-and-decrescendo stuff. (Try paying *really close attention* to Stars of the Lid or (oh god) Godspeed You! Black Emperor sometime. Not easy.)

Maybe it was the millennium. No really.

Admittedly I was in college for a couple of years on either side of the Y2K anticlimax so it all just felt sharper brighter more becoming-finally than usual; and yes maybe the real border between the slow god☞state melt of the Euro-millennium and whatever joyless antimodern death-obsessed theocratic counter-revolution we're now muddling amid was the morning of the 11th of September, 2001; I'm not so sure but OK; OK but didn't it seem, wasn't there really that feeling, that Weird sense (at least artwise, at least here) that something immense was coming? Movies, music, new forms coalescing online and in streets, glitches in the Matrix or like the man said *Pre-Millennium Tension*...remember? If you're 30ish or better you came up at a weird time, your kid stuff was 80s toy tie-ins and by the time you lost your virginity it was pills and robot music at 250bpm *minimum* to get you there...hip kids played at being children while their parents bought mail-order Viagra subscriptions and were *underwhelmed* or perhaps distantly *preoccupied* with Waco, Ruby Ridge, Seattle; or they stocked up on ammo thinking rightly Something New Is Now and their kids went off on Phish tour to get away from all that shit.

Maybe Jerry was the Rope of the Norns after all, not General Patton, and when he went away the Midgard Serpent really did awaken and slide (all scales and eyes of blood) into Denver to see the show, or even play, I mean it *looked* like Pete Wernick up there but c'mon, it was *dark* in the McNichols Arena that night wuntcha say...

Not to say this was Serious Business though it sure felt that way if you let it. Not as if SDS was putting up fliers on Shakedown[13] at each tour stop. The Suicide Club was up in 77 and down in 83 – maybe you weren't even born yet and I was still pissing myself at Pre-K. The Dead were antimodern too in their way, huh? And they were long gone by the time the young bloods rolled into Colorado thinking 'damn I wanna hear that funk tune again, Katie or something, how's that go…' You're not dangerous if senators turn up for your funeral. Not allowed to be. Or they name an ice cream flavour after you…

I mean it's easy listening for white male stoners born too late for the Dead and too early for sexting. *This is not important.* No revolutions left.

♥ ☞ ❊ ☞ ✳

So turn inward. Every transformation starts with the Self – I'm not sure that's true but it feels nice to say, like 'Love conquers all' (which is both trivially false – gravity always wins – but true after all in a loopy way, as maybe Love is the single human process or behaviour or generative energy-transfer that can most widely and deeply affect the others; but come back to that later). Maybe it's better to say that social transformations can only *take* when coupled to parallel personal transformations: tiny individual changes can generate startling movements in the aggregate,[14] but given how easily *perturbed* we are, sustainable change (maybe just eventually?) always rides on back of larger-amplitude private change…

So turn inward. It's only a rock'n'roll show after all, and maybe it's enough that when the house lights fade and Kuroda's

---

[13]'Shakedown Street'==the vending area in the lot near the venue, where the kids on tour sell glassware and grilled cheese sandwiches and the politics of the moment. The whole thing's named after the Grateful Dead song, without irony, which should tell you something about our little fan culture's bold move forward into cultural self-creation. Whatever.

[14]http://web.mit.edu/rajsingh/www/lab/alife/schelling.html

lighting rig flares bright Technicolor and the noises around you freeze into human shapes (or I guess when the people you're with, the one(s) you are, melt into noise) you enter into a new state. You make new rules.

Revolution in the body.

Phish shows provide *unbelievable* sensory overload – not just tinnitus-inducing volumes of sound like every goddamn concert nowadays, but Chris Kuroda's outlandish *improvised* light show, that inescapable mix of sweaty human and burnt-plant smells, the press of nearby bodies…it's nothing like the antiseptic experience of listening on headphones in your home (like I'm doing right now, Timber > Simple to kick off the second set; I just killed a moth). Half the appeal of such an experience is its *inescapable* sensuality: you're very much caught up with your fellow humans at the show, particularly smooshed together in that small space right in front of the stage but really no matter where in the arena you are. There's nowhere to go and nothing to do, really, but dance; no one forces you to move but you'll have a much easier time of it if you do, not least in avoiding the spasmodic 'dancing' of the dude next to you…

And of course the key to this pleasurable overload is first off the sensory *deprivation* that precedes and enables it. Same with going to the movies, compared to television: in the dark with lots of anonymous people, getting sensory information without context (like being tickled in a blindfold), your audiovisual senses ascendant, subconscious movements marking time, above all a feeling that your comfort in the physical environment will be provided for so that your psychic space can come under a kind of consensual assault – we enter into such places (contracts) to experience very literal *psychotropism* (mind-changing), assured of our providers' benign intent. What if god could promise your safety after sunset – would you wander? Would you dream further out if you knew you'd be able to welcome in a world of no worry, afterward?

TV is domestic. Head-sized heads in your living room, stories about doctors cops firemen and high school students singing about true love. 'Normal.' The movies are bigger than life: bodiless and placeless, you're greeted by 20-foot-tall giants beaming grand emotions and booming voices at one another (at you, *in* you). It's like having your sensorium directly interfered with, as scary and maybe amazing as that sounds. (You can even do it stoned if you like.)

As soon as cop and detective shows made it on TV, the movies could start treating those figures with all the ambivalence of hushed private conversation. ('I don't want to seem…well, you know…but sometimes I can't help thinking…') Movies are about *danger*, and about *relief*. They scare you and then comfort you.[15] You go into the dark to receive the Light. Ever been to church? Same thing. Easter Vigil, the Paschal candle, robed wizard leading tuneless chants: 'Christ our light…light of Christ…light…' Then the lights come on and something new can be born. The year. Believers.

My friend Norah came with me to the 2010 Great Woods show. Afterward she said the jamming seemed 'manipulative' – quiet gathering, steady climb, joyous peak, drop rinse repeat. I should've asked if she still prayed, if so to whom, if so why, and how did it feel (regardless) when no answer came. What in the *world* could be more manipulative then opening yourself up totally and taking that moment to *lie* to yourself about the most fundamental truths…on the other hand, why get defen-

---

[15] The smaller the movie theatre, the less likely you are to be comforted afterward. Phish fans, draw your own parallels here.

sive about it? Praying works just as well as dancing, if you work at it. It keeps demons away for a while. Lights go down, lights come up, unexpected order is revealed, no setlist, a keening electric sound fills the room, someone is at your elbow, a friend is dancing with you to music a stranger has made, *the truth is the movement…*

The entire second set of this Denver show seems to be accompanied by that weird guitar loop. 'Psychedelic' you wanna say but what does that win you? No never mind, it's not drugs I'm hearing. It's prayer. Tamboura drone. *Permission* (which is welcome). Not manipulation: just rise and fall, like breath.

It's easier to laugh with other people, and to cry sometimes. That's what this music is for! So you don't know what's next and you welcome everything. The guys onstage are going through the same thing, when the music's right, and everyone is safe to be new together. Isn't that nice.

❤ ☞ ✿ ☞ ✽

Tension and release. That's all this is. When to tense up. How to let go.

❤ ☞ ✿ ☞ ✽

1997 was a great year for fans of the song Harry Hood, which has always featured a standard-issue broadening crescendo to a joyful major-chord climax.[16] I'd say much of the song's appeal

---

[16] Bowie, Slave, pre–1997 YEM, Mike's Song, Black-Eyed Katy, Taste, Suzy, and Reba all have more or less the same dynamic contours. Rule of thumb for fan reactions: if the band takes a smallish harmonic/rhythmic left turn (an unexpected shift to relative major, say, or smoothing a three-chord jam out into one sustained chord plus spacey sonic effects) during one of these tunes to create additional *tension*, but manages a tight unison return to *release* that tension on the good ol' downbeat, fans will gobble it up. Manageable unpredictability. Just like the stock market, or *Law and Order*, or Mommy carrying Baby.

comes from what Mike(!) once derisively referred to, if memory serves, as its 'predictably New Agey D major jam': you always know just where it's going and pretty much how it's going to get there.

Phish stopped ending the song with an emphatic unison shout (cf. *A Live One*) in 1996 or 1997, and the change took *something* away from the tune even as it allowed band and audience a smooth descent from the jam's climax and an extended cooldown before the next tune. This change was in line with an overall shift toward a more fluid, continuous, holistic approach to dynamic set construction, away from the group's somewhat combative early/mid–90s comic perversity; though there's also a certain indulgence there. I love 1997-era Hoods for their *sound* – like everyone else, Trey cites *Loveless* as a favourite album, and I feel like there's a straight line from Kevin Shields's[17] sonic sculpture to Trey's late–90s rhythmic-ambient experiments. Hood was one of the tunes that directly benefited from this new approach in Fall.

The Denver Hood is a classic, building from silkspun hush to roaring primary colours by way of Trey's bravura lead guitar work. In its cloudy sonics and simple lullaby-like melodic lines this Hood prefigures the sculptural Philly version from early December, and shares DNA with several beloved 1997 jams, from the Vegas Stash to the Darien Hood, not to mention the huge Timber jam that kicked off the second set just 40 minutes prior. It's a *shapely* performance: the band sets out to do one difficult thing and does it, seemingly without effort.

---

[17]Let us take a moment to recognize what a miserable shit Kevin Shields has been to an enormous number of collaborators and friends, and to acknowledge that his 'perfectionism' is inseparable from both his creative achievement and his serious mental health issues; and let's give thanks that Phish consists of four pretty happy, healthy guys who've maintained a great friendship and partnership over several decades despite experiencing emotional crises aplenty.

Trey is prone to what some fans cheekily call 'TreyDHD,' a tendency to try and grab *all* his ideas at once and squeeze them into a set or show or even a single solo, which can make for jarring discontinuities or frustration for fans looking for smooth continuity first and foremost. He's always done well with Hood, which opens out into a languorous I-V-IV space and stays there a good long time; still, in his dual role as ornamental lead and architectural rhythm player, he doesn't always arrive at the final *huzzah* in one piece. But Trey achieved an impressive degree of relaxed focus in late 1997, stepping back from his lead role for long stretches and letting the band's democratic improvisations take solid shape before moving into his customary topside melodic position.

In the Denver Hood Trey strikes a delicate balance: his guitar curlicues have a singsong clarity and simplicity even as they template the band's ensemble movement. All four players achieve real lightness here, particularly Page, who builds an electrifying dissonance around Trey's single-note thrusts late in the jam, only to bring the whole thing crashing joyfully down at the close. Dig Page's I-IIb pushback against Trey's glowing major thirds in the seventeenth minute, and his surefooted sidestep into cheeky blues a moment later – Page is doing an enormous amount of work here within a 'simple' three-chord jam! But Trey has the conn here: pushing the whole band into a martial build in the fifteenth minute, filling the upper register with fog to shift rhythmic focus to Mike and Fish, ascending (over three or four minutes!) the long major chord thirdwise to provide a series of plateaus for collective gathering and upward explosion. Mike and Fish empathetically mirror Trey's combination of upper-atmospheric haze and precise rhythmic punctuation, so that his lead guitar line never seems like a solo, but rather a element of some ongoing evolutionary process, a sand castle emerging from the shore as a topographic inevitability, a principle, instead of (say) clumped bucketfuls stacking, stuck together…

Of course they close with Izabella, which isn't anticlimactic so much as much (?) of a muchness, and maybe giving away the game entirely: I mean, in those days sometimes the fifth man was James Brown, invisible onstage, but for a *lot* of November and December 1997 it was Jimi Hendrix, as the phrase 'upper-atmospheric haze and precise rhythmic punctuation' shoulda made clear, *duh*. A soaring solar Hood doesn't really need another tune to follow it, but if the set isn't yet spent, it makes sense to build on Hood's governing sonic principle.[18] The Hendrix cover is just an alembic – it purifies a key ingredient.

❤ ☞ ✤ ☞ ✳

OK, my derisive footnote about the 'interesting' lyrical inversion in Bug reminds me: You might say there's nothing actually secret about Phish's very complicated music – its wisdom is *exoteric*, on offer to everyone who comes into the temple – so organized Phish fandom is there to provide the requisite mystifaction. Hence ratings, rankings, ego-stuff of every sort.

It'd be nice if the word 'display' worked schematically, *dis+play*, meaning the opposite of play, or as an alternate spelling of some

---

[18] In later years Trey would grow inexplicably fond of following late-night Hoods with Bug, an impressively bad song whose closing jam – really a guitar solo – is *all climax*; it always feels to me like a musical cheat, a way of buying back the triumphant feeling of the Hood jam on the cheap. Hood is a misty mountain climb into sunrise; Bug is like looking at a postcard of that mountain while listening to the last two minutes of the Hood jam over and over and over again. Though on the other hand it's 'interesting' that Hood builds to permissive pleasure at its climax ('You can feel good, good, good about Hood') while Bug dives straight for the Dark at the End ('It doesn't matter, it doesn't matter, it doesn't matter').

hypothetic *dys-play* ('disordered play')(!!). But no. It's just anglicized French for 'unfurl.' Which OK *maybe* you can get away with pretending there's some link to 'erection' there, with attendant semiotic complexities, but (as mentioned) no. No, no, no.

Something about the fandom runs off at unpleasant angles to the thing itself, the music, the Great Attempt. About *my* fandom too.

> Jafsie was a shadow figure in the Lindbergh kidnapping. He volunteered to act as a go-between, and may, in fact, have been part of the crime.
>
> John Henry fought the steam drill through the mountain, and, through that his momentary victory, established something other than the extent of his pride.
>
> Perhaps Jafsie was a criminal, and perhaps John Henry was a fool.
>
> I offer these essays as examples of my search for a new model.
> (David Mamet, *Jafsie and John Henry*)

NOVEMBER 17, DENVER

I: Tweezer, Reba, Train Song, Ghost > Fire **II:** Disease > Oblivious > JBG > Jesus > Circus, YEM **E:** Char0

It's amazing that the 16th, with its odd rhythms and dark blue light and all-encompassing haze, and this beloved show, best known for upbeat jams and dance rhythms, came from the same band.[19] The emotional and stylistic distance between the two shows is one of the best indicators of how far the band traveled between their most famous mid–90s show, the New Year's

---

[19] 11/17/97 is available as an official release, *Live Phish 11*, which I strongly recommend even to non-fans.

Eve blowout at Madison Square Garden in 1995, and their radically different month-long peak in Fall 97.

Phish were famed for their professionalism and *consistency* in the early days, not to mention their catchall nerdiness, which made a stylistic/generic buffet out of every show. That's half the reason they never caught on, if you ask me. (How do you recommend a band that's guaranteed, at *every single concert*, to play 30 minutes of a kind of music you dislike?) 1997 was the first year where a single musical style dominated Phish's live shows – no tongue-in-cheek cock-rock covers or perverse onstage improv exercises intruded on the hypnagogic mood – and the stylistic focus made room, paradoxically, for an emotional richness and intensity quite different from the old days. Having suppressed his desperate desire to entertain everyone in the room (e.g. with fussy setlist construction), Anastasio found that he and his bandmates could bring the whole crowd into an intimate emotional space by playing less, *planning* less, and staying with emotional impulses instead of trying to exhaust them and move quickly on to the next Neat Idea.

Which is why something like Mike's acoustic miniature, Train Song, works a little differently here than in its previous setlist appearances: instead of a musical maneuver or display, it's an emotional consequence of the tense, restrained, 'anticlimactic' Reba jam preceding it.[20] In a set with one teary-eyed prog tune, two gnarly funk jams, and a howling Hendrix cover, Train Song makes perfect emotional sense – trees along a nightroad come to deathly life with tearing fingers and wooden teeth dripping

---

[20] The Caspian and Ghost jams from Hampton just four days later produce that same extraordinary tension, and like the Denver Reba they find release only in the anthemic jam (there a 25-minute AC/DC Bag, here a Ghost, or *the* Ghost maybe) that follows. Same with the excellent Seven Below from Star Lake, 6/23/12, which takes three different show closers to fully dissipate.

sapblood, but for a moment the moon peeks through to whisper reassurance. All part of the scene.

♥ ☞ ♣ ☞ ✳

This Ghost is one of the purest expressions of joy in all Phish's 1997 catalogue. The climactic movement is nearly identical to the famous 12/30/97 Bag jam, and has the same feel (especially in Trey's guitar work) as the distended, hazy half-hour Ghost from the IT Festival (8/3/03). It nicely illustrates another shift in Phish's musical approach: from steadily ascending melodies and 'machine gun Trey' trilling away at the major third to cap every feelgood jam (check out the *Live One* versions of Hood and Slave) to *climactic grooves*, not just attaining but maintaining emotional states. Dig the Star Lake Gumbo from August 13 (or the famous Worcester Hood from 12/28/10) – the audience goes nuts not for melodic escape but for tight polyrhythmic interlock. Instead of peaking, the music progressively *deepens*, as the musicians focus on the moment rather than the movement beyond it.

If you're thinking this sounds more like 'duration music' and electronic dance music (EDM), give yourself a gold star. After the Denver Ghost's signature jam crests and rolls back, its primary-coloured straight eighth notes and singsong major chords give way to a new groove with a hint of batter-fried swing to it, and the band effortlessly brings the jam to *another* climax, Black-Eyed Katy's aggressive male cousin. Which gives way in turn to a third groove, its woodblock punctuation and clav/wah texture prefiguring the darkly ecstatic Izabella > Twist transitional jam that'd hit Detroit on December 6…Trey twinkles atop spare, spry midtempo skip from the other three players until deciding to flare out with a set-ending take on Hendrix's Fire.

Telling moment: he prefaces the Hendrix cover with a little speech:

> Thanks. We're gonna have a lot more music for your dancing pleasure (and listening pleasure).

It's considered bad or weird form to parenthesize spoken text, but just *listen* to the recording – it's clear to me that, maybe for the first time, he's seeing what the group is doing as *essentially* geared to movement rather than the cerebral engagement Phish's improvisation had theretofore always required.

The second set moves away from this purely kinetic focus but keeps up the smooth mood-modulation that characterizes both good techno and good improv; it's very much the second segment of a continuous perceptual/experiential arc. Note that this could *only* happen to a band working without a setlist – it's the emergent emotional formations that dictate the band's movement within and between improvisations, rather than a preexisting, necessarily *abstract* conception of the music's character.

You can tell it's all unplanned – Johnny B Goode would *never* get scheduled right after the very similar Oblivious Fool,[21] which emerges from a combination of the pounding DWD groove and (perhaps) Trey's apparent need to turn away from a tiny mistake at the end of that jam, to stay in the groove and make up for its anticlimax. (He plays the closing DWD riff an octave lower than normal, doesn't quite manage the usual triumphant hosedown that ends the DWD jam, and steps back into a chopping rhythm snarl that modulates neatly into Oblivious Fool.)

---

[21] …unless a guest star were onstage, in which case the stylistic envelope is invariably tightened to make the guest more comfortable. Standard, really. Note that with few exceptions, Phish's guests tend to amplify the fun of the live show and restrict the free flow of the music itself. Good *conventional* musicians get lost easily in Phish's continuous four-way exchanges.

The 35-minute DWD > Fool > JBG run has to exhaust itself in loping midtempo electro-haze before the second half of the set can begin: a laggardly Jesus Just Left Chicago, Los Lobos's melodramatic When the Circus Comes (three covers in a row!), then finally the band's signature tune, the icy prog-to-funk crazyquilt You Enjoy Myself, complete with tense whisper-quiet final jam.

The new requirement is emotional coherence and intensity. Even the smiley-face tunes burrow deep instead of popping off. Even the sad ones seem glad of each other's company.

❤ ☞ ✻ ☞ ✳

Even during pregnancy my wife placed great value on punctuality. So did our son, apparently: contractions started at midnight on the due date. She asked for a playlist of long instrumental tunes to help her relax and defocus during early labour, which can be a time of mounting impatience and frustration for the mother. I chose mostly early–70s Grateful Dead. She seemed to like it.

On the other hand, she doesn't like to hear those tracks anymore. Three notes of the Watkins Glen soundcheck: 'What is this? Is this the labour playlist? *Come* on.' I love her as much as anyone or anything on earth but this saddens me.

She was in labour for 36 hours. It was difficult and she was extraordinary, as women are called to be in such moments. Well, the three of us made it.

It was the *best* day(-and-a-half) of my life.

But it wasn't the happiest – nowhere near it.

To be sure, the moment our son emerged from his old home into our world was blissful release as intense as I'd ever known; I felt fully human as I never had, and though diminished, that feeling remains; but the pain and fear and encroaching madness

– a night, a day, another night, and a long morning – make wistful remembrance impossible. My beloved was *hurting* for a lot of hours, hurting as she never had, and try as I might, I didn't do everything I could to ease her suffering, or even her pain. I think I was a good and comforting partner throughout the process, in the main, and she has reassured me on that score. Our son is happy and healthy. But...

The point of this excursus is that a state of bliss, of total *egoless presence and openness*, needn't involve pleasure as such – just as suffering is an opinion about pain rather than an extension or consequence of it. Taking LSD was one of the best decisions of my life, and years later I feel like I'm still mapping the memory of that extraordinary day, but I don't think I was 'happy' at any point while on the drug. The feeling, instead, was of intense multimodal *reality*.[22]

For once I was out of my own way, aware of connection rather than isolation, *allworlds* rather than my own protagonist Self-obsession.

Phew, for a minute there I *lost myself*...

❤ ☞ ♣ ☞ ✻

All of which is the long way 'round the barn to saying that the end of 'What You Want' by the Rolling Stones is perfect, maybe the single most climactic climax in all of rock'n'roll and one of the few moments I'd wrap up in a box for my inevitable desert-island exile...but life goes on even after the final note has faded.

---

[22] If you read this and snicker, thinking 'LSD is the *opposite* of reality,' you should consider whether that reaction anything to your own happiness – or to anyone else's. Maybe read up on framing psychotropism as 'alternate' versus 'altered' consciousness. *Zen and the Brain* is a nice place to start, if you're sci-cool. Well, William James will do nicely as well.

And the phrase 'life goes on' should scare you as much as it comforts you…until you (we) see it as without colour or slant, as a plain fact like 'books have words' and 'Jesus was a man,' and let ourselves rejoice in mere truth. Things as they are. The thingness of things. Bliss is honesty.

I quite like this version of Ghost, as much for its failure to transcend as for its willingness to just boogie on. It just is.

> If we are not fully ourselves, truly in the present moment, we miss everything. When a child presents himself to you with his smile, if you are not really there – thinking about the future or the past, or preoccupied with other problems – then the child is not really there for you. The technique of being alive is to go back to yourself in order for the child to appear like a marvellous reality. Then you can see him smile and you can embrace him in your arms. (Thich Nhat Hanh)

honey, come to a phish show

- S: 8/13/97. Not 'honey,' speaking strictly – rather my best friend in high school, modulo my brother of course – though after the show S and I were finally candid with each other about years of complexly building romantic feelings. She loved the show (how could you not? Gumbo goddamn!) but had to miss Darien the next night. I don't think she stayed a Phish fan. I just remembered: she gave me my first Phish tape. 8/20/93, Red Rocks, just the first set. With an adorable custom j-card with a Phish logo on it. An important gift.

- J: 4/5/98. Holy mackerel, what a show! She had and has a talent for being immediately, deeply happy with whatever bullshit she's doing. Even me. Can't last forever and didn't…but in one of life's charming little ironies, I called her a few months ago and she said she was at *yet another* Phish show – Atlantic City I think – with some dude. Whodathunk.

- V: 9/11/00. Goddamn, or was this 9/10? And in any case V was very definitely not 'honey' here or at any time, *much to my fucking chagrin*. I was bored out of my mind at the show. First show I ever saw drunk, if memory serves.

N.B.: not worth it. Booze isn't the ideal drug for a Phish show.

- A: 2/26/03. My ladyfriends were lucky in the shows they attended. Superb show. She didn't like it. We argued the whole way there, as I (mis?)remember it. We lived together for a couple years around this date. Shouldna. Most of what went wrong is on me.

- L: 8/13/97, 8/14/97, 8/1–3/03, etc. I'm a terrible friend so this may feel…gestural? demonstrative? but let me say here that my girl Laurie is one of the best people alive and she and Tarkanian, a chap and so excluded from this roster, are the two human beings I most want to see Phish with — my wife is out, see below, and my son is too young to deal with the marijuana smoke. Seeing Laurie dance to Silent in the Morning on a torn ACL at Darien Lake in '97, tears running down both of our faces, is one of my most cherished bittersweet memories. She handled the entire drive from Boston to IT in a broke-ass VW van that, if god existed, She'd have struck that shit down as a blasphemy against the idea of the automobile. Perfection.

- Am: 6/19/04, 8/11/04. One of the all-time greatest 'see with a romantic interest' Phish shows and my pick for best of '04 and the tickets were a gift from her but it was all too too something and I don't know that I was capable then of love and some days I wish we'd never met. For her sake and mine and the sakes of several other people mentioned here. The August show at Great Woods was shit, shit, shit, shit, shit. Not her fault!

- Agi: 6/6/09. She's game but not a Phish fan. I'll accept

that someday. Plenty of chances, god knows – she's my wife. Sucker! Note that we married *before* Phish reunited. She had no way of knowing what she was getting into.

and furthermore

NOVEMBER 19, CHAMPAIGN

I: Julius, Gin > Llama, Dirt, Limb, Bitch, Theme, Ginseng, Fee > Antelope **II:** 2001 > Wolfman's > Makisupa > Taste
E: Possum

My phish.net review of this show, in its entirety:

> Very strong first set, but the second is…well, just look at that ridiculous setlist. It's *that* good. I think. The Wolfman's > Makisupa made it onto the official 11/17 release as filler, and it's a somewhat tense but nonetheless thrilling ride. (Trey has one of his I'm-the-boss,-follow-me moments in the middle of the Wolfman's jam; what follows is worth it, I suppose.) And you can't go wrong with a deluxe set-opening 2001 in the post-Went intergalactic funk mode. The Hampton and Denver shows get more love but this one's a heck of a party.

If you can extract any value or meaning from that then you are to be congratulated. Who's the reader-in-mind, there? Someone who can read a setlist like that and know its implications (two funk tunes, a reggae coolout, and a quasi-Latin jambeast in the second), but apparently hasn't actually heard the show. What? How would you attain the prior knowledge necessary to parse my review without hearing enough of the goddamn music that you *don't anymore need the review?*

This may seem weird but I actually sought out the 11/17 *Live Phish* CD release just so I could hear the Champaign filler. The second or third time I ever went to my first college girlfriend's house in Rhode Island – whoa, was it during the Island Tour? – I commandeered her tape deck and, presumably as 'ear training' for the show, threw in this fan-favourite 2001. (It's not really called '2001' but it's way too late for us to be worrying about such things.) I can still picture the j-card from my tapes – there's hardly any text on there at all! *Four songs* over 66 minutes in the second set, not the first or last such set but still a revelation to me, the first such set I'd heard Phish or any other band do.

The above-quoted phish.net review is dated 10/20/09. I'm writing *this* on 8/11/12. Nearly three years on I can't quite generate the same enthusiasm for this show that I once did. 2001 is gnarly downtempo perfection, parts of the Wolfman's > Makisupa reach deep space, and the perormance quality is the same as pretty much everything else on the tour...but as another phish.net reviewer puts it, 'If there's a knock on this jam and this show, it's the fact that Trey sort of does his own thing during parts of Wolfman's, without listening to the rest of the band.'[23] In general Trey's Fall 97 moments at the forefront came in the context of either traditional solos (e.g. Chalkdust) or 'space jams,' those obsessively circling guitar spirals that rose up out of the rhythm bed to paint the sky and then dissolve into some new thing – but Trey's angry left turn during the Champaign Wolfman's is something else again. Instead of open-minded assertion, it's a *boss* moment.

Not to say the speed-rock jam that follows, recalling Llama and Crosseyed & Painless, isn't diverting at times. It's interesting to hear the group gather itself after the leader's weird intrusion,

---

[23] http://phish.net/setlists/?d=1997–11–19

try to put together a coherent jam, then fight its way to Makisupa Policeman; and this is one of the deeper Makisupas they've played. Plenty of meat on that Taste as well. But it's a few different things from top a-bottom and you can't go back from *A Love Supreme* and *In a Silent Way* and *OK Computer* to the grab-bag, you *can't* damn it, or if you can (I guess you can) then please somebody tell me how. I miss thinking there was such a thing as innocence, and finding this shit funny.

♥ ☞ ✿ ☞ ✳

A note about Trey's 'oh look at this nicely set table and this friendly-looking family gathered around having a nice time at maybe a holiday dinner, LET ME TAKE OUT MY COCK AND PUT IT ON THE TABLE' moment roughly eleven minutes into this Wolfman's jam:

This is little different from what he does when he calls for a new song, especially in Phish's post-setlist practice. And it's Trey's job in the band to kill tunes that aren't working out and steer the ship between songs. What's disappointing isn't Trey's insertion as such, it's the fact that the jam is clearly sputtering a little bit at the 9:00 mark, and dissipating by 10:30, but it could conceivably have evolved into something interesting at that point…and there's *nothing* interesting about the music that Trey chose at that point. The interest (as I've already mentioned) is in hearing the band try to reassemble itself, and just not quite managing it.

That's much of the fun of improvised art – the way the logic of assembly is explicitly offered to the audience, out front, as part of the experience (rather than ideally kept invisible by hoped-for emotional effects).

No but while we're on the subject of girls[24] let's talk about the basement and the campus coffee shop. Halloween 1997, The Slip played at MIT's Senior Haus along with the Miracle Orchestra: two Boston-based jazz/jam bands, Phish acolytes in a way. They played for something obscene like five hours altogether. My man Colyn and I danced with this pale cute pre-med student with shoulder-length light-brown straight hair, the kind of hairstyle smart women sport who have opinions about girls who get by on sex appeal, and we were of course completely smitten. I will say that I was wearing a dress at the time and was still thin, unmuscled as I'd remain, with curly unkempt hair and more preconceptions than experience and I was maybe even cute in dim enough light but surely not desirable and hadn't yet learned the difference. I almost miss it. (Almost.) We danced 'til we were falling down and then walked across campus in the bearable wee-hours New England chill to the student-run coffee shop, where we talked until sunrise and she mentioned that she had a boyfriend, and we were, as some guys can be: so so proud and excited to have experienced so *magnificent* a disappointment.

I tell you that to tell you what comes just after this: I've seen the Slip on pretty much a yearly basis between that night and two months ago, always in Boston, and they're an obscenely talented band with a gifted and sensitive songwriter/guitarist, but they bear *almost no resemblance* to the band I and Colyn and the quietly lovely mousy-brown-haired girl saw just over eleven years ago. They used to be a true 'jam band,' with a more specifically jazz-based vocabulary than Phish and a much more sparse sound but very much in that mold; now they're a stylistically-

---

[24]The rest of this section was written in 2009, as part of a 20,000-word essay which you should be grateful I'm not forcing you to read, Reader(s).

varied indie-pop band and I can't even describe it. Go, just go, but what I really want to tell you is this next bit. In maybe 1999 I went to see The Slip at the Somerville Theater, on my own, and during the song 'Yellow Medicine' a group of revelers came out onstage in enormous school-mascot costumes – pink bears, birds, great big neon-green monsters – and when the song's final chorus came crashing back after the thumping percussion solo and delicate restatement of the melody, the singer *screeeeeeamed* at the top of his lungs instead of singing that one final vocal line. And even cold sober (whatever that means) I started jumping up and down as high as I could, hands clamped on the back of the theater seat in front of me, and – who knows – but I'm fairly certain I was screaming at the top of my lungs too. I remember nothing about the show but that scream and those dancers. I was absolutely overjoyed, the way you maybe immediately want to jump back on the roller coaster after that first nervewracking ride of the day, when you realize that the thing won't kill you and that no one holds it against you that the deception has *worked*. You were always supposed to be scared, and then to find out you had nothing to be scared of; the revelation and the terror are part of the same aesthetic continuum, linked overtly by mere *time* but connected at the root, hidden underneath the skin of earth by some deeper nature.

Which is to say, you're supposed to ride the roller coaster once *and* you're supposed to ride it *twice*; the thing contains both modes of being, there's no canonical experience being dissipated or merely echoed the second time around. See, look: I thought I was gonna die, but I was never gonna die; then when I knew what was up, I looked for the feeling again, the bliss of *not* knowing. But I never *really* thought I was gonna die, nor did I ever quite get over my fear – I'll shake like a leaf next time I get on a coaster, as ever. New every day, or night; and the same every night, and day.

The imaginative act of keeping these two seemingly contradictory or desires – tension and release – in mind at once, is the reason to be there when the lights go down. Everything won't happen, but anything might, and the *chance* is the thing. It's the water. Its depth is a function of trust and skill and all the other stuff your piano teacher or softball coach or writing instructor used to harp on; mechanism and meaning aren't the same thing but each is found in the other. Tension and release aren't the same thing but each becomes the other. Or to turn it around: the imaginative act of keeping seemingly conflicting desires in mind at once is *the act of love*. It is faith.

❤ ☞ ✱ ☞ ✲

In other words, it's OK that the last tennish minutes of the Wolfman's jam kind of suck. It's OK that pain happens. Disappointment is something that you *choose to make*; it doesn't happen to you. It comes from inside. If this Wolfman's Brother makes this Makisupa possible, and of course it does in some sense, then I'm glad for it. I always thought the doofy reggae tune was *stupid*. It is! Jesus, of course it is. And it's also the ice-glass shards where this show's heart should be.

I was going to say 'but' but 'but' is an editorial about 'and.' Colyn and I were genuinely happy to have wanted something we could never have had.

He read *Ulysses* in high school and actually *got* it near as I can tell, so fuck that guy. Still. Nice story, I thought. About the brown-haired girl and one perfect night.

Oh I remember. Her name was Joanna.

♥ ☞ ✿ ☞ ✱

There's a musical fragment Phish used to perform, more or less a straight-up King Crimson quote, which they still tease from time to time: Dave's Energy Guide.[25] It's not complex music, more a counting exercise: just a series of odd-time circular patterns from each player, building tension through maddening repetition and the mysterious disappearance of a downbeat. (For many folks, one synonym for 'tension' is 'incomprehensibility.')

The phish.net setlist file says there's a DEG quote in this Taste. Maybe so, maybe not; I don't care in any case. I want to talk briefly, instead, about this Fee, which gives way after its final refrain to a gorgeous interlude – delicate harmonic patterns and upper-register twinkle from the guitars, gentle piano arpeggios alongside, a little bit of Latin syncopation in the drums. For maybe four minutes the band floats and circles this way, until Page's synth chords arc across the stage and clear the air for Trey's patient segue into Antelope.

Absolutely top-shelf stuff, this.

I mention DEG along with this passage to illustrate one of the abiding principles of this music, of a certain kind of art: the tone and indeed *purpose* of DEG couldn't be more different from this sweet jam, but they're both machinic-minimalist passages which build in volume and density to a specific kind of emotional uplift (or in any case culmination).[26] The band's ba-

---

[25]Invaluable listening guide here: http://doggoneblog.com/2010/04/12/what-is-daves-energy-guide/– that blog is one of the few useful, musically-literate Phish websites, by the way.

[26]In the last episode of *Buffy the Vampire Slayer*'s fifth season, Joss Whedon uses the word 'arrived' as a euphemism for orgasm; I've begun to think of that choice of word not as a cheeky substitute for 'came' but as a generous accounting of the purpose of sex. We go somewhere together, wait for each other, are glad of the journey and grateful for the rest. Did I say 'the purpose

sic unit of improvisation isn't strictly groove, here, nor harmonic movement – more generally you might call it the *situation*, a set of harmonic/rhythmic/melodic starting points and implied (but mutable) constraints which the entire ensemble is operating simultaneously to strengthen and to dissipate. The tense gnarl of Dave's Energy Guide is an end in itself, but it's also setting up something none of the players can yet anticipate – they're all looking forward in the music, but they won't step off without each other. It only works if they're all together.

The genre of the music, in other words, is less important than the ensemble movement within it. Hence the stylistic scatter of albums like *A Picture of Nectar* and *Rift*, which fans nonetheless experience as a kind of continuous musical consciousness – the movement logic is consistent from song to song.

Once you learn how to listen to all four musicians at once, and to hear also the music's fifth element, the hidden pulse to which they're all also responding, your relationship to other musics becomes more complicated.

♥ ☞ ✤ ☞ ✳

I've been listening to a bunch of Ornette Coleman lately, plus my usual semidaily dose of electric Miles Davis, and today I dove into some of Pat Metheny's gnarlier stuff (he does indeed get gnarly, including on *Song X* with Ornette, in places one of the most beautiful things I've ever heard).[27]

---

of sex'? I mean 'bliss.'

[27] If you've never heard Ornette Coleman, this is a great album to start with; on several tracks Metheny paired written harmonic structures for improvisation with Coleman's effortlessly beautiful melodies, yielding an interesting hybrid music that's accessible but still wild. 'Endangered Species,' the 13-minute centerpiece, sounds like a chaotic assault, but with a readily graspable polyrhythmic skeleton and an almost minimalist logic of construction – distinct movements made up of short repeating phrases, with a three-way shooting war breaking out in the rhythm section. Awesome.

It's hard to write about Phish's innovations, which I do believe are real, when confronted with century-altering geniuses like Ornette and Miles; and it's hard to take seriously a description of Phish's improvisations as 'free' when Metheny's going apeshit on The Calling or Endangered Species. Ornette's 'harmolodic' conception offered a good deal more rhythmic and harmonic freedom than Trey's/Phish's open-ended, open-minded rock groove approach, less obviously coherent but able to reach unbelievable heights of complexity and richness. The Haden/DeJohnette/Denardo C. rhythm section really does *groove* like a twelve-headed beast on *Song X*, too.

Listening to, say, the 12/29/97 Cars Trucks Buses after spending time on 'proper' jazz is disorienting: Phish's structural coherence and great empathy are impressive, but the harmonic material is so unsophisticated by comparison that I kind of want to crawl under my desk. (Jumping into a mid–70s Dark Star afterward is equally weird – the Dead's rickety rhythms, literally incoherent ensemble movement, and harmonic jumble mark them as neither jazz fish nor rock fowl.)

Yet Phish's ability to run simple harmonic material through detailed, complex dynamic/rhythmic/structural variations – to *maneuver the entire band like a single solo instrument*, in a way – is uncanny. I've never heard another band that could move the way Phish moves on (say) the Champaign Limb by Limb, and that's still just a monotonic crescendo from sweet sparseness to primary-coloured climactic anthem: it's Phish 101, not yet approaching the intricate ambivalence of the Denver Timber or Johnny B Goode…

Which is why I'm *not* embarrassed to jump back and forth between Phish and electric Miles Davis. One thing I don't hear from Miles's (superb) early/mid–70s electric bands is continuous dynamic movement and structural transformation – OK, so that wasn't what he was going for, but shows like *Dark Magus*, the famed Isle of Wight set, or even the comparatively fluid *Pangaea* generally feature discrete sections with relatively static dynamics. Check out Miles's solo in the middle of *Pangaea,* disc 2, or the abrupt transition in 'Calypso Frelimo' (a favourite jam of mine) on *Dark Magus*, or the extremely rich but arguably starkly bipolar Isle of Wight set (e.g. 'Spanish Key'): these bands are capable of deep grooves and heady atmospheres, but it's hard to get away from 'OK let's establish *this* groove *now* and X, Y, Z will solo in that order and now it's time for a discrete step toward the following, 1 2 3 4...'

Look, Miles's funk/rock albums[28] are some *sick shit* without question. Phish have never grooved this hard or wailed this *nasty* in their entire lives. (How many bands ever have?) But Phish are out to solve a different problem using some of electric Miles's tools: how much rhythmic and harmonic freedom can you give a four-piece rock band while maintaining total dynamic/structural cohesion – cathartic downbeats, welcoming structure, *collective* coloration always the goal no matter what harmonic material is in use...?

In any case I feel tension between my desire to boost Phish, who after all do achieve something night after night that other bands can't for the life of them put together (three hours of music that blends challenging composition and expansive four-sided improvisation in equal measures, drawn from a library of hundreds of songs with no setlist, usually producing a music of *exceptional* improvisatory coherence), and my awareness that for

---

[28]What else do you call *Dark Magus*, if not the broad term *rock?* I'm not sure 'jazz' is a better name, though that's the shared harmonic language; those punishing drums on 'Wili' ain't jazz, period, and what Pete Cosey (RIP) does with his guitar on that album is 23rd-century science anyway.

all their great musical value, their achievement is arguably a *narrow* one. What Phish do feels different in kind from other improvised music, but arguably they differ from (e.g.) rough-and-tumble 60s/70s jazz collectives mostly in *degrees* of harmonic complexity and rhythmic cohesion.

But even as I write this, I'm thinking of the next two shows in Hampton, the riotous AC/DC Bag and the rocketlaunch at the end of Halley's, that nightmarish Caspian, the way Ghost melts down into a pool of dark dreamstuff nightlit from within…

I'll have to settle for this: there's a family, an academy, to which Phish's music belongs (and which it honours), and I can't yet name it. That's one of the goals here. Thankfully it's not the *only* goal though.

❤ ☞ ✽ ☞ ✱

Last thing before moving on.

> Herbie Hancock has this thing about an informed vocabulary but a childlike approach. He plays simple, simple, catchy melodies, but all his chord voicings have forty or fifty years of this theory in them. So when he gets onstage it can be all childlike. Not childish. But if you ever stopped a Hancock recording and looked at a few measures of what he's playing, you'd be floored. The voice leadings are filled with all these ideas. It doesn't sound complicated, but it's a more mature, elegant palette of emotions. These guys can hit an emotional chord that a lesser player couldn't. It's the same way a great writer with a great vocabulary can bring out subtler emotions. (Trey Anastasio, *The Believer* interview, July/August 2011)
>
> If you charted the course of harmonic progressions in the biggest radio hits from say, Elvis to now you'd watch a steady shrinking of tonal movement. There are good musical reasons for this! I hasten to add. But at this point, **we can't**

> **take any more harmonic information away**. Harmony that moves through keys is nonexistent in most current indie rock, radio pop, and hip-hop. (*my emphasis* –wa.) (Reid Anderson, 'Same As It Ever Was')[29]

One element of this story that's always appealed to me, resonating with my various neuroses and preoccupations, is the way the members of Phish in 1997 reached new levels of emotional expressiveness by reducing their music's complexity. That transformation is related to Trey's comments about Herbie in the *Believer* interview: instead of building complicated structures, mature players use their technical tools to support risky *emotional* movement. The brainwork stops being the point of the endeavour. I get flak from fans at the phish.net when I say there's almost nothing in pre–1995 or pre–1997 Phish with the emotional depth of the later music, but 'high on their own abilities' doesn't count as deep emotion, and the band had never really gone *dark* before the autumn melancholy of *Billy Breathes* and the weirding rituals of mid- and late–1997…

At the same time, as I write these essays I'm remembering the many times non-fans have told me that 'the jams all sound the same,' which is one aspect of Reid Anderson's observation above. He's right to couch his complaint in terms of quantity of *information* rather than 'beauty' or 'meaning.' The music of Fall 97 does run together somewhat – this is especially true of the fan-favourite Hampton shows – and it's not surprising, in retrospect, that after stripping down the music's formal complexity in 1997, the band (especially Trey) began to focus on its purely sonic character in the last years of the decade.[30] In part

---

[29]http://dothemath.typepad.com/dtm/controversies-woody-allen-david-byrne-herbie-wayne.html

[30]Some fans call this the band's 'millennial' style of jamming; it'll do. In the months leading up to the millennium show at Big Cypress, Trey hit on

this was a deliberate choice, a way of continuing their experimental approach while staying accessible…but there's a hint of desperation to Phish's 1999–2000 music too, as players and audience realized how few tools the rhythm-centric approach had left them with as improvisers.

I'm willing to bet that most of the band's *hardcore* late–90s fanbase actually got into Phish in the mid–90s or before – so did I – and those fans experienced the hypnotic simplicity of Phish's ambient/cowfunk experiments not as a musical style unto itself but as a solution to theretofore-unseen *open questions* in Phish's performance approach. I think that's part of the reason Fall 97 is still held in such high esteem. Phish's journey from the maximalist roar of December 1995 to the minimalist insinuation of 1997 is personal. I take it personally.

And thousands of young people could undergo that same transformative cycle for the cost of a nightly ticket. Less, even, if they could sell a few grilled cheese sandwiches in the lot after every show.

Hell, you could turn a profit *and* act the part of the boho bodhisattva, if you bathed with fashionable infrequency and had a decent drug hookup.

I'm starting to see – maybe you are too – that talking at sufficient length about these rock'n'roll concerts is a way to talk

---

a sedimentary guitar approach reminiscent of 1997's 'space jams' (cf. 11/14/97 Twist, 11/22 Halley's, 12/6 Tweezer), with clouds of distorting effects and feedback enveloping an aggressive maximalist attack. The rhythm section was tighter than ever, and jams would roll skillfully through the fog for 20 minutes, less various than of old but producing an intoxicating, enveloping effect. (The NYE 99 Sand might be the all-time classic jam in this style.) While Trey was playing a lot more then than in 1997, individual notes almost didn't matter to his approach. Sound was everything. It's the closest the band ever came to 'laptop rock' in a live setting, unquestionably impressive, powerful…but Big Cypress was surely an endpoint for their development in this direction, and it took them a decade(!) to figure out a new musical identity.

elliptically (or not so much that) about Us. Our country of the imagination. In moments of egotistical weakness, that turns into talking about me, and I apologise.

But that's where I hear the music, you see. That sound rolls across the topology of us (remaking the body in its spectral image) and afterward we carry it away echoing inside. I can't even hear it in itself anymore. The ringing sound is part of me now. We're the resonator, aren't we? I'm the house my old self lives in.

NOVEMBER 21 AND 22, HAMPTON

I: Emotional Rescue > Split, Beauty, Dogs, PYITE > Lawn Boy > Chalkdust, Caspian **II:** Ghost > Bag > Slave, Loving Cup **E:** Guyute

I: Mike's > Hydrogen > Weekapaug, Hood > Train Song, Billy Breathes, Frankenstein > Izabella **II:** Halley's > Tweezer > BEK > Piper > Antelope **E:** Bouncing, Tweeprise

My entire review of 11/21 from the phish.net, if that's OK – to set up various themes, seed your ears with some minor thirds…

I'm an unapologetic Fall '97 booster, fanboy, partisan, evangelist, and myopic egotist – i.e. I insist that Fall '97 is the best of all Phish tours, partly because it's my favourite…though I also insist that it's my favourite because it's the best (see above re: 'myopia' and 'egotism').

But some things are worth going crazy over.

(The following is occasioned by the long-awaited official SBD release of November 21 to 23, 1997.)

The fandom responded ecstatically to the tour at the time, as you'd expect; among other things it represented a sea change in how the band approached show structure (never mind the pornographic music itself) – some folks were convinced that 'there [were] no first sets anymore,' and given that this show kicks off with a 20-minute funk workout, it's easy to see why. Time has been kind to the tour as well. With the benefit of hindsight we can see how Fall '97 began a darkly generative period for the band (their imaginative freedom nightblooming even as their technical command and professionalism began to falter amidst a rapidly decaying backstage/fan scene), while representing a historic peak of possibility and intensity. With only a couple of exceptions, the band was just absolutely *there* every single night, taking song after song to deep dangerous places.

It was a good time to be a Phish fan.

The best jams of 2011 – R'n'R at the Gorge, the Tahoe Light, the brilliant 'elements' set at UIC – seemed to draw some of the same dark energy that powered Phish's late 90s music: layered textures, intricate polyrhythms, effortless group interplay, soaring ambient passages, guitars put to unholy new uses, keyboards much abused, drums caressed and then shattered. Above all, the music flows now almost as it did then, with extraordinary patience and organic inevitability.

But what's missing from Phish 2011 is the black ice that became their premillennial music's center: cool austerity of early 'cow funk,' anxious chaotic 'space jams,' the *scary* quality it had. (Hear the way Izabella comes roaring out of 12/6/97's fog like an angry undead stowaway, or the teeth-gnashing mania of the Hartford Char0 > 2001. A lotta Hendrix in the air, then.)

For all the expansiveness and ambition of the band's Fall '97 work, the tour feels All of a Piece; it all belongs together, the maniacal Hampton/Winston-Salem stuff and the knives-in-blacklight Worcester jamming and the retro-dufus-turned-pornstar goodtimes in Dayton and the astral lullabies in Utah and, and, and oh those sorcerous goings-on and splashings-crashward in Auburn Hills (cloudpiercing peak of a deepwater volcanic island). The same can't so much be said of the new music; ironically, as the band's palette has grown to include more lived-in sounds (and whatever eerily the goddamn 'storage shed' jamming is, when it eerily ever is), they've lost the glasseyed focus of back-in-the-day. They might sound like any number of great bands these days, even Zeppelin a bit when the moon's right, but there was something harrowing and deeply pleasurable about knowing (walking into a familiar room, strangers at close quarters in the dark) that the approach was gonna be, ready set go, THE METERS AND PINK FLOYD ARE TRAPPED TOGETHER FOREVER ON A DERELICT SPACESHIP ALL ECHOES AND GHOSTS AND ALONE AND THEY ARE SAVED FROM COLD DEATH ONLY BY THE COSMIC-IRONIC FAVOUR OF PLUNGING SLOWLY INTO AN OCTARINE SUN, GAINING SPEED, FALLING, HOLD ON…

To the matter at hand.

Emotional Rescue isn't a great choice of cover beyond its novelty/comedy value – the jokey falsetto and sparse texture wear thin some time before the jam starts – and the jam does feel like a show-opening warmup, which of course it is. But 17 minutes of shambolic Phish funk (climaxing in a transitional few minutes of lovely dark ambience) is a fine easygoing thing, regardless. And it leads into a very nice Split, for which we supplicants are naturally thankful.

Et cetera et cetera, and Caspian (a tune tailor-made for smoky indoor-venue AUDs, by the way) is a strange but appropriate choice for a first set closer: excellent version here, particularly Trey's digital-delay offering to Hades in lieu of those closing rock chords from the album, which…

1. ...fondly recalls the beloved 12/31/95 Mike's, and...

2. ...helpfully signals to the crowd that we are setting our course for darker night in Set II.

The show's back half kicks off seven consecutive must-hear sets (next breather: 11/28 I). During Ghost the players bail on that song's basic funk patterns in favour of a haunting spare passage typical of Fall '97: minimalist assembly, assured group rhythm work, and a patient crescendo and sighing wavebreak into a wry, spry midtempo jog at the outro. 1997 is THE year for Ghost, but this performance trades its standard snap/pop/wah funk for something moodier and more meaningful.

Then yeah, a true segue arrow before AC/DC Bag, and *get ready* for this Bag. Less decisive and authoritative than the canonical 12/30/97 version, but also less linear, the 11/21 Bag takes a few minutes for somewhat clumsy I-IV thrashing (a climax too early, it seems) before settling into a deadly take on the introductory PYITE groove. Fishman slides to the ride, Page leaps onto piano, Trey sprinkles some space-jam fairy dust over everyone, and suddenly we're working a slightly ambivalent variation on that I-IV, posing as Triumph while whispering Collapse, Dissolve...and after a twinkling ambient passage, we return to ambivalence: minor-melancholy rock clatter and swerve, Page's piano diagonals zagging at everyone else's zig, or I guess vice versa. 25 minutes of top-shelf Phish, and another true segue into Slave.

Slave, as you'd expect after the foregoing 50 minutes of music, is devastating. Well, it's a 1997 Slave; the mycological languour[31] of late–90s Phish was well suited to tunes like this one.

---

[31] Someone said reading my blog was like 'mainlining a thesaurus.' I get such comments all the time. *Fuck that shit.* If you know what these two words

More Stones to close, of course. They've always killed on Loving Cup. And is there a better, more coherent long-form composition in Phish's catalogue than Guyute? Pure prog mayhem in the encore. Nice.

...

11/22 gets the press, 11/23 gets the 'underrated masterpiece' tag, and of these now-forever-conjoined triplets, 11/21 is the li'l sibling with – hey whaddaya know – some earth-shaking powers of its own. I think you can pass on this first set without feeling TOO bad, if you really don't think you can spare that hour of your life, but that's a swell half-hour you're missing at the opener, and a ringading Caspian to close. The second set, meanwhile, is as good as Fall 1997's usual, which is to say it's a solid hour of deadly focused improvisation, favouring eventide melancholy and dissolution, crescendi desperately imploding or exhausting themselves in gouts of terminal noise, minimalist funk with a mischievous dancing step and slow poison on its blade, visible in the right kind of dark...

Ego-costumes aside, in the end it doesn't matter whether Fall '97 is the 'best' Phish tour. (One hopes the best is yet to come, right? What kind of person *doesn't* hold that hope, or pretends not to?) Those are fun arguments to have, but it's all just circles around imaginary selves, signs that read No Trespass: there's no place for borders like those when the music begins. I'll say instead, quite confidently, that on these nights 14 years ago, Phish reached the windblown jagged top of one peak, bringing thousands along with them; several other peaks would follow,

mean – 'shroomy drowsiness' more or less, now you know – then it's either a good precise evocation of the music's feeling or not, but if the writing has any value, if you trust me at all as a writer, then looking up the occasional unfamiliar word is really the *absolute minimum* work you owe the experience. (Not me. Your own reading.) I didn't write this to show off.

as several had come before, but this one had a Weird light, and everyone why got up there saw something extraordinary. And would you believe it: it's still there. Might I recommend heading up alone some night. Go on: follow the strange glow that won't fade. The dark will keep you warm.

❤ ☞ ✤ ☞ ✻

In a less fannish (generous? apologetic?) mood, as I've fallen into since coming down with *hand foot and mouth disease*[32] 9ish days ago, I might be heard to say that 20% (70%?) of the Hampton run is bullshit. Maybe more. Tweezer is aborted by Trey only after it's already petered out into gesture; Bag takes a *long* time to get going; the Halley's jam is completely static for its first seven or eight minutes, just like Mike's Song, just like the *interminable* Emotional Rescue opener...

And it's not like these are bad examples of Fall '97 shows – 11/22 is *archetypal*, with its headlining space jam and funky/ambient opening frame and obligatory BEK/Piper. If you wanted to explain this moment of your life to a non-initiate you could reasonably just hand them a joint and a muddy audience recording of this show and call your work done.

So why bother? On the face of it, this music is *middling*: it's good-not-great funk, thoroughly *precedented* ambience, no one particular thing really. It's the Big News of our best band's best tour, the two-day D-Day of late–90s rock music, and they

---

[32] You don't want this disease. Lesions in the back of your throat make swallowing into medieval torture. Your whole body aches. Your hands feel like burning all the time. Your heels break out in spots and walking is agony...I got it from my toddler, and I'm *glad* he got it now rather than later, because the lesions didn't itch for him; the only problem for toddlers is trouble swallowing. (We ended up in the ER at Children's Hospital with a dehydrated baby, but a few hundred mL of saline solution later and he was as happy as any child has ever been – tired but entirely restored. Even his fever broke fast!) Now he's immune to this strain for life. Lucky boy.

can't even wring sixty seconds of interesting music out of goddamn Tweezer, one of the most reliably Interesting Songs in Rock since, like, 1994! What the *hell*, Trey.

♥ ☞ ♣ ☞ ✳

Needless to say this is a minority report – and I've apparently decided to be 'quirky' by copypasting a hazy hagiography in front of this contrarianism, or do I mean *confession*...

No one hates these shows. I don't think I've ever read a bad word about Hampton 97 in *ever*. I commented on the phish.net bulletin board that I was considering the idea that the Hampton 97 shows are overrated, and one of the resident wits responded in full:

> lol noob

OK then.

Trey likes to open shows with a warmup tune, and both Emotional Rescue and Mike's Song seem designed solely to fulfill that need: dead-simple midtempo grooves, goofy singing from Mike, a chance for Trey to very slowly work up to full speed on the guitar. An immensely long monochrome rhythm workout whose hidden subject seems paradoxically to be impatience...or else I'm projecting, maybe even hoping the band is as irritated by the fantastic banality of each night's opener as I am.

Folks *love* these jams, by the way. If by chance you don't already know,[33] Mike's Song has historically been a histrionic

---

[33] Who are you? If you're not a Phish fan, how did you make it this far? How can you possibly know enough to read these essays but not have heard this music, or need to read a meandering 'guided tour' through a bunch of 15-year-old live concert recordings? The harder I think about this question the more frustrated I get; to stave off despair and get the project finished I'll leave it aside for the moment.

two-chord rocker, its jam section famously split between a nasty F#m cock-rock jam and a more freeform second section in F. In 1997 the band gave the first leg of the Mike's jam a cow-funk makeover, sometimes replacing Trey's hush-to-roar blues moves with a silky Gumbo/YEM/Ghost/Wolfman's groove and sometimes doing away with the midstream key change entirely. The Hampton Mike's is a perfect example of the song's late-90s form: instead of one of Phish's patented long-form crescendos, the jam rises up out of quiet by getting more expansive, its rhythms more tightly interlocked, its upper atmosphere a wash of electronic haze, clacking percussive patterns losing form in the roil…

And it goes on and on and *on* for 17 minutes, cresting and receding instead of spiking a discrete climax. Almost the opposite of the band's longtime method, I'd note, but the rhythmic consistency is absolutely perfect for enshroomed dancers, or some lacrosse-playing East Coast trustafarian[34] in Izod lightly perfumed with rubbish beer trying to remember where his girlfriend is waiting on the lawn, if she and his other accessories are being properly *maintained*…same with Emotional Rescue actually. Just one plodding groove for (huh) 17 minutes, and a Weird-ambient bridge to a considerably more engaging Split Open and Melt.

So what's the value of this music? It's not like the four mem-

---

[34] While giving a mini-lecture on semiotics in a sociology-of-media recitation at Tufts I suggested that Bob Marley's image in pop culture had nothing to do with the man or his music or (heavens no) his politics and had become a free-floating signifier (yawn) meant to notify visitors that, Yes, We Smoke Weed in This Dorm Room. An angry-looking white dude with a buzz cut and a Raiders cap said he had Bob's poster up in his dorm room. He then told me he was a Rastafarian. After confirming that he really did believe that the former emperor of Ethiopia was God and Bob Marley was one of his prophets, I switched to a different lecture topic. The most irritating, embarrassing thing about the event, from my perspective, was that I'm right about the fucking posters; Raiders Cap is the exception (to most every claim ever made, apparently) that proves the rule.

bers of Phish stopped being their hungry experimental selves for the duration of the show; and most of this music is accomplished improvisation, much of it highly detailed, all of it at least fun if you're not me...what's going on, here?

♥ ☞ ♣ ☞ ✻

Possibly the only good thing about iTunes vs my late lamented gorgeous rather too expensive dual-well cassette deck (miss ya pal), is that I can see, say, Phish's entire Fall 97 Tour – or Radiohead's discography, or the Atlantic Ornette compilation *Beauty Is a Rare Thing* – not as individual albums/shows but as a stream of single songs, hours and hours of tunes flowing seamlessly together not even as sound (you still hear one second per second even in the promised all-digi all-tha-time era) but as *poetry*: I mean the list of song titles and my memories of them actually come together like a rhymeless schizolyric. I love it. Means the break between *Kid A* and *Amnesiac* goes from illusory-anyway to *gone*; or John Zorn's *Book of Angels* albums become one interwoven thing like they surely always were in his Weird brain; or, or I suppose *and*, I can flow quite smoothly if I'm not paying attention from (say) the filler on the official November 17 release (the Champaign Wolfman's > Makisupa, grrrrrr) to the Hampton Emotional Rescue opener, which feels like a creative step *back* in some irritating indefinable way. To me. No, that's not the good part. The good part is being able to see and *read* the shows one after another in space, to see song titles and durations up against one another and be reminded that what I think of as timeless, 'Fall Tour' allways, represents in fact 21 shows over exactly one month, and Hampton/Winston-Salem is a three-day Mid-Atlantic run before the descent into darkness that is the tour's climactic New England sequence.

I can hear the band getting…bored?

I'm projecting. Let's go with it.

The two Hampton shows, the crown jewels of the tour in so many fans' memories, are the purest examples of what we take to be the canonical Fall 97 sound. Plodding swamp funk: check. Prickly bitonal guitar/rhythm interlock: check. Psych-anthem 'space jam': check. Sonic haze thickening to opacity; distended chemical comedowns; a constant ironic twinkle, like a concealed bell tinkling merrily as death's door opens: check all. Hell, they had such a good time playing Black-Eyed Katy in Hampton they busted it out again in the very next set, which they never ever do. It's an *exhibition*.

But maybe there's no movement here. Eerie ambient sound hazed up off the desert floor and those disco-dweeb grooves coalesced in the mountains, but there's an angry howl in that Champaign show, and Hampton is like a retreat from that destructive energy. Or a vacation; I mean, it's *great music* in the sense that it is purely itself.

See, but the whole tour turns right over in the *next* show, the one after the One and the Other One, Sunday in Carolina. This is Friday and Saturday – would you believe I never gave even a single instant's thought, prior to a couple of years ago, to the way Phish shape their performances for weekend vs weekday crowds(!!) – and there's a party on. And *only* a party.

My confession (we're packing up our apartment, I should be in bed to rest up for the final push, the lights are so low I have to confess something) is that while I usually listen exclusively to the show in question while writing one of these goddamn essays, I've moved ahead to the hallucinatory insanity of the Carolina show while drafting this bit. Trey's Hendrix exorcism.

It's supposed to climax here. Y'know, we should be talking about the two sides of Fall 97, the patient galactominimalist space grooves of Hampton and the animal wail of Winston-Salem, blah blah, and how 12/6 at the Palace (oh we'll get there) represents one of those once-in-a-lifetime moments when everything the musicians were capable of, they delivered with perfect egolessness and joy, blah blah, unifying both halves of the tour or something…

I can't though.

I'm not where I'm supposed to be; in my head I sound like another Self.

inside outside

The following was written on March 10, 2010 in Anna's Taqueria in Davis Square.

You can retreat into your own head, if you're lucky. Dark and quiet and cozy. A shell for hiding and containing you. We're not all lucky though. The inside of my head is sometimes the noisiest place on earth. I don't just mean the ringing in my ears – tinnitus it's called – which makes perfect quiet impossible; *thoughts* are the problem. They rustle when they move and they're always moving. For one thing it's all words: 'someone said' this, a song is 'stuck' in my head, or I misremember something and before you (I) know it it's a part of me. Someone said you can't see except to *see as*. Sounds right. Thoughts get in your eyes. Feeling are colours; a bright enough colour blots out all lines. Strong enough feeling and it's all you can see or hear. In my head there's no difference between sound and sight. It's not a place after all. ('My mind' is an idea my mind has.) When I listen to music I can dwell inside it, under the umbrella arc of a melody or in a shadow that's chord-shaped. But within my skull some other diabolical physics applies; nowhere to hide, bright light gets everywhere. Or should that be 'metaphysics?'

I have to retreat *from* my head. I feel like the figure and I feel like the ground. So I was walking one day, I must have been, and saw a horrible face with my inner eye, or it's horrible to remember it anyhow; that was years and years ago but he's still there. I noticed he was a part of my mind, I suppose? Jack, he goes by. Or that is the name I gave him at that moment; or his dead face grew like a cataract around the words I saw. 'Jack dandy, Jack dear, Jack is the devil and *now he's here…*' And here he is. How could a face contain such a smile? Was he a part of me before I knew it? Did this body, *mine* I insist, coalesce also around the notion of me? Was I made of mist once as he was, or of memory?

But if he didn't whisper it would go quiet and still, and it'd be nothing but the ringing in my ears. It seems someone has left my handset off the hook. No more signal, just noise.

There was *no* sound, then a loud one, and now just a quiet one. Quiet not gentle. I hear the broken electronics that made me go. Their bye-bye song. Robot broke. Okie-doke.

But if I welcomed the thoughts themselves this would be fine: the noise, even. If it were music I'd bear it. What it is is imbecile whispers. A snatch of something too small to be music, four notes, say, or even worse the image of some dread danger at the foot of my bed, or the back of my mind. Some devil's face. Inner noise so loud it *shakes me*. I think if I wake at night in the ghost minutes and ghoul hours before dawn, as blue ink creeps back into the sky, and if you hold me, you'll feel it. The rolling surf sounds overlap, catch and cross at time's axis, the very sound of zero, and a hum begins to spread through me, louding and fastening. I feel it in my marrow. The sight of it painfully loud.

A clatter and wail, ricocheting off a cement wall. It was music but too loud for me to discern its shape. Just a wall and a wall and I felt it afterward. For hours afterward, deafened. Then just broken robot parts. That was the thing that killed me. Some capacity was written away like unwanted words in a letter. Shhhh.

Hush now: zipzipzip tssss ftftft pop. Ffssssss. Little sounds, little feet, tracks on the inside of my ears. Goblins walking around in there.

My dialtone moans dully now at a frequency that might have carried messages. Music, even. Forever and ever I will be hearing this. Halfwit.

But that quiet space, horizontal line cut into the graph of all I hear, is no respite. The quiet is bad and the noise is bad. The quiet is part of the noise, as you breathe the same air the fire does.

Trying to talk about thoughts and we keep coming back to noise. Every colour of light makes white; every colour of ink runs down, down, downhill to pool in black. That's what it feels like: all this noise runs together into just shadow. There's no difference between what I think and what I hear and what I see. I am these things, the shattering wave upon the wall, the darkling accident of colour.

I'm the whole weakling world, feels like, the dreadful stuck song fragment, and the light is deafening.

That's what it feels like inside my head.

♥ ☞ ❦ ☞ ✳

The following was written in February 2009 in the Starbucks upstairs at the Harvard Square Coop and hopefully it will explain why writing the previous fragment was one of the scariest creative experiences I'd ever had.

I experience a mild form of synesthesia whereby I see melodies and chord progressions as blocks of colour moving through space, defining a kind of spatiotemporal domain or a density gradient. I literally see the staff sometimes and notes parading across it – not notes so much as *ranges*. Clouds even. OK, I have a tough time describing it. It's linked to my ability to transcribe and rearrange music intuitively (i.e. I can usually hear a tune and write down its chord progression the first time out, improvise accompaniment right off, and then give you the chords in all twelve keys without much labour). I know that music 'makes sense' in part because the accompanying visuals depict a kind of lock-and-key mechanism, or sine waves coming into phase, or confluent shapes close-packing like crystal molecules. I mention this not to brag – near as I can tell it's an innate characteristic as meaningful as my height – but to suggest that this might be a good *learned* framework for listening to improvised music in general. The musicians' work, in jazz and other improv, is to provide the soloist or lead player with a rich framework, a conceptual baseline from which to move out then return. Hearing the music as a field, a conversation, the *transmission* of thought (electricity), lets you get past the big hurdle for many new listeners to improv, which is **it takes forfuckingever and doesn't make a lot of sense.** The language of jazz is its own world, sure, but more importantly, improvisational *practices* demand a mode of listening, specifically of *acceptance*, quite different from e.g. the procedural language of classical music. And good collective improv asks one extra thing, which is that you live *without satisfaction* for some length of time as the players work up the structures that in written musical forms would be givens – premises.

Musical improvisation at its best embodies an evolutionary model of punctuated equilibrium: good ideas get rewarded quickly, but even off-the-cuff notions play out, have ripple effects, make room for ecstatic outgrowth as well as slow conceptual interpenetration. (They learn to live both joyously and with one another.) Ideas are *not* precious; the goal of the organism isn't survival, it's propagation – the survival of the *gene*. (The 'meme' if you're a hipster.) Darwin, Freud, and Marx all had versions of the same extraordinary idea, basically that complex systems can evolve something that resembles intentionality even in the absence of a Prime Mover, a first object. God doesn't have to be real for the world to *look* like it, in other words. When improv gets going, there might be an overarching structure to the proceedings, but it doesn't have to be there right out, nor is it something the players come to, a destination. It's an emergent property, connecting both forward and backward in time; it's a characteristic of any honest creative activity. 'Artistic' coherence is mainly a characteristic of work done in good faith – work that gets out of its own way. Which if you're a novelist doesn't mean your characters are real beings living inside of you and dictating the shape of their story and you should write according to whatever whim strikes you, *oh God please don't no no no* – only that the categories of your imagination have an integrity that most expressive vocabularies are inadequate to translate, so the way to let ourselves do great work *without* needing to spend a hundred years in solitary contemplation and practice is to find a form that lets us listen first and then speak meaningfully. To escape the tyranny of our own voice by pressing it into *service*. I'm not agitating for the restoration of the military draft or anything; this is an essay about (sort of) rock music, and nothing is less rock'n'roll than the goddamn military draft.

❤ ☞ ♣ ☞ ✲

This bit's new.

Magic is real, of course.

It's *not* the invocation of a divine or spiritual force; there's no deity to be contacted, nor can the dead speak to us in the sense 'clairvoyants' and mediums claim. (The dead do speak, of course, as books and gods do: through us only.) If what you want is a magic spell to 'make someone love you' just give up; it doesn't work that way. But love spells do work if you remember that the key component is the *test*, the followup appointment: approaching the loved one with confidence and humility and a spirit of seeking. That'd be the magical act, in case you're wondering; the rest is algebra.

Tarot cards can't tell the future but you can make a future sitting there looking at the cards. And some of them are very beautiful: which is to say they're an invitation. Beauty is something we become. (Look *at* the cards if you like but what you're looking into is: duh: a question.) Ayahuasca doesn't put you in touch with another plane or demiurge or whatever you might wanna call it, LSD either,[35] though obviously something touches something; maybe I mean that casting the spell is bringing one mode of being (thinking?) into careless contact with another. You're the field and the lines of force. And the jungle isn't a holy place unless by 'holy' you mean 'wholly without pretense,' a state of utter mereness, in which case you could save yourself the cost of the plane ticket and just volunteer at a local library. Or just *stop lying to yourself.*

When I say 'magic is real' I mean a few things at once, and none of them seem even slightly contentious or complicated or weird to me. Radical shifts in consciousness obviously have the ability to change the essence of a human life – and the right ritual act entered into in the right frame(s)[36] of mind can, and every-

---

[35] The discovery of the psychotropic qualities of LSD by Albert Hofmann is, for my money, one of the happiest accidents in the history of science, and a paradigmatic(!) case of 'paradigm shift' if you're looking for one. Great intellectual leaps forward often consist of little more, at first, than extending some object's list of interesting characteristics by one.

[36] Yes, multiple mindframes at once. *Of course.* Isn't that the point of this book?

day does, induce such a shift. Divination doesn't do what it says on the tin, but it obviously does *something* – something closely tied (again) to the consciousness of the petitioner. There are no ghosts, but *people do see ghosts*, just as auditory hallucinations are labeled 'the voice of God' (cf. famous epileptic writer Saul on the road to Damascus). There is no 'macromind' in the doofy New Age sense of human intentionality residing in a great body made of human bodies (plus maybe plants?), but the network phenomena we call 'thoughts' find easy parallel in the collision of memetic objects from stories to stupid digital images of cats with 'funny' captions written on them.

A rock band can't show you God, but whatever 'seeing God' actually *means* at the physical level – and billions of people have experienced just this phenomenon even though it's not real, just like most of the Western world has imagined Hamlet or Jesus – a rock band can get you to that place. If they're listening hard. Y'know they *sainted* John Coltrane, somebody did. Because of the songs he could hear and say. He was a magician if anyone was. And as hard as it is to listen to some of his solos, I mean an hourlong 'My Favorite Things' would tax the most patient listener *goddamn*, but as hard as that is, the music is welcoming too. Its emotional logic is clear, its formal structure transparent. Trane is *there* for real.

Eventually you stop hearing the playing and become aware, really deeply centrally aware, of nothing but the music, which is to say the path the sound takes through your mind. Music isn't sound: it's listening. The way you listen. See what I mean about magic? 'Abracadabra' doesn't work; believing it works is what works. It won't stitch together the magic box with the lady inside cut in half. It'll accomplish something much more impressive: without changing a single 'physical'[37] fact or object, it can change the expectations and perceptions of every single person in the theatre.

God is exactly as real (and as mad) as King Lear, and believing in Lear has helped me through some rough moments, not least the death of Cordelia, so who am I to say you shouldn't believe in God? Whatever 'believe' means here.

And so then what does it matter whether the Hampton shows are better than XYZ, or good, or 'static,' exist in or out of time, piss someone off, make you cry, are perfect background music for when people of a certain highly specific temperament and shared cultural background fuck, are the midpoint of something (maybe just my freshman year of college or yours), get 'funky,' fall short of Winston-Salem by one or another standard, mark a turning point for Black-Eyed Katy though the canonical version is Carolina's…

For a year I served as a fulltime stay-at-home dad, and sometimes when my toddler would refuse to sleep in his crib we'd go for a drive down Storrow Drive and out to Soldier's Field Rd and back over to the Science Museum, a few miles of smooth road, plenty of gentle turns to sway him easy to sleep…on the stereo to begin, the same thing every time: minute six of the Hampton Halley's Comet. The monotony he needed to zone out and cool down, his carseat's sunshade shrinking his world to a V4 rumble and midtempo funk groove in F – and a treat for me, music I actually liked. I got really, really familiar with that jam over those hours of driving. *Halley's > Tweezer > BEK.* It took us both somewhere, different places but together. Two guys who trust and love each other. I was working as hard as I possibly

---

[37](in the narrow sense, i.e. excluding mental phenomena which are as physical as electricity)

could, exhausting every physical and emotional resource I had to keep my boy happy. Which is to say it was bliss – I was fully human.

When I say magic is real, that's what I mean; that's magic; not the music putting my son to sleep, but the feeling of total humanity that came of a shared ritual born of generosity and love and welcoming. We need each other.

He turned two years old this weekend and doesn't sleep in the car anymore. And now I find the Hampton shows a little boring.

> And I believe in the future
> We shall suffer no more
> Maybe not in my lifetime
> But in yours I feel sure
> Song dogs barking at the break of dawn
> Lightning pushes the edges of a thunderstorm
> And these streets
> Quiet as a sleeping army
> Send their battered dreams to heaven, to heaven
> *Paul Simon, 'The Cool Cool River'*

♥ ☞ ✤ ☞ ✲

My first show, Niagara Falls, December 1995. Fred's there. He says 'OK I'm gonna go make out with this glitter chick some more.' In retrospect I know exactly what he means. They play a huge Mike's Groove with no breather tune in the middle, no Hydrogen or Leprechaun or Simple bliss. It's lost on me – I haven't heard Mike's Song or Weekapaug Groove and don't know what to expect, i.e. how to be surprised. How deeply. They played a bluegrass tune. I danced in the great big open space between the mostly-empty bleachers and the general admission crowd. It felt a lot like a pep rally. People were spinning like wobbly tops, I didn't know why. I'd never seen people on psychedelics dance (or anything) before. Otherworld. Something was called into being, or more likely we were called, all of us.

No line between those formal features and these, and 'Hampton,' though of course it's the same musicians, same vision, same welcome. Or the formal continuity is there and someone is going someday to need to talk about them, maybe to students, maybe it will have died and laid to rest in a museum by then but right now it's far too much the morning, I helped speak my son to sleep in our family bed by reciting *Goodnight Moon* ten times (again) as my wife held him close; and I can hear the line between here and there. It has nothing to do with form, really.

Hearing back to then it's like I was *enveloped* by something. By sense. Multisensory overload, but not just that, this feeling that everything was of a piece: purple light, glitter girl, thunderous noise from the stage, what I now know to be a weird little delay loop jam in the unfinished Weekapaug (I'm almost glad I can't remember the actual music; it's enough to be able to regenerate it, to revisit such deep terror…). The world was one thing very purely made and all its senses were bent toward that single being.

I'm not quite getting it.

I felt like I'd walked into a temple and someone handed me the sun.

> nobody is truly sane until he feels gratitude to the whole universe
>
> Oscar Ichazo

From my essay 'In the tomb I become,' summer 2010.

You can connect through space, through shared purpose, experience, activity, identity – even through time. If the present day seems somehow oppressive or (how myopic) unlivable, you can escape into days already gone by, and make of the past not only a simultaneous presence but a replacement present. In those years I discovered a wellspring of extraordinary American music and started to perceive the outline of a continuous cultural history. Its essential element was risk, which is to say faith: I saw that brave artists had midwifed new worlds night after night in hidden rooms and consecrated spaces across the country. The rites had gone on for decades and continued even then, and now.

I wanted to be there as it happened, but even more I started to enjoy seeing how it had previously turned out. The old forms that experiment had taken. To take refuge. Live tapes are to live shows as religion is to belief, and that was OK with me. I was too much the thinker in those days to allow belief to make me less alone – a task to which religion is perfectly suited. The task, indeed, for which it was designed.

Kids who went on tour with bands always annoyed me. 'Irresponsible,' I'd say to myself, and I'd walk around Boston late at night, through medieval alleyways, bustling hotel lobbies, the dark wooded Esplanade. 'The nerve of dropping everything to go off alone like that,' I'd say to myself. 'Lucky bastards.' I refused to envy them – sometimes even aloud.

...

I sometimes venture a wish to rejoin that circle of care and preservation. A line of men and women once happily took up the task of preserving a time and place in the history of this country. They had no charter or obligation, built no institutions. And as it happens, no one thought to preserve in turn their own rich culture. The rites that raised the temple. The tapes are around, sure, but they only contain the *music*, know what I mean? You can serve others (even imaginary others) or your Self, I suppose, and I'm moved by the idea of that generation of archivists laboring on behalf of some idea of All of Us Together, an expanding and exploding greater self – disappearing into the great work, dancing to mark the passage of the Dead and of the everliving.

♥ ☞ ✽ ☞ ✳

The woman who came with me to the last night of the Island Tour split up with me around a year later. It was the right move from her perspective and was good for me too, though of course I couldn't have told you at the time.

We began breaking up sometime in late winter or early spring 1999, and finished the job in August.

I mention that in case you were wondering what happened to the Hampton review. Some things take time. Be cool.

and furthermore

NOVEMBER 21 AND 22, HAMPTON: REDUX

I: Emotional Rescue > Split, Beauty, Dogs, PYITE > Lawn Boy > Chalkdust, Caspian **II:** Ghost > Bag > Slave, Loving Cup **E:** Guyute

I: Mike's > Hydrogen > Weekapaug, Hood > Train Song, Billy Breathes, Frankenstein > Izabella **II:** Halley's > Tweezer > BEK > Piper > Antelope **E:** Bouncing, Tweeprise

What's the method, here? 'Tribal' drumming/chanting, for one thing: harmonic simplicity, minimalist polyrhythmic assemblage, endless spirals of music building in density and intensity without needing to get louder. Shades of afrobeat, funk method beyond funk content, barbershop[38] tunes; ripples showing up later in the music of Animal Collective, Wilco, Bisco… bluegrass echoes too, with a song's movement consisting sometimes only of its arrangement filling out. And the Dead, yeah

---

[38] Barbershop singers achieve extraordinary gains in intensity of sound through the sly use of inversions and especially mutual resonance – matched mouth shapes that turn each of the singers into each other's resonator(!), making for remarkable sonic coherence when everyone's in tune. The final 'tag' of, say, Sweet Adeline or Hello My Baby is meant to generate this effect; Phish just can't actually do it, though they get a million effort points for trying. If you've never heard such a thing, track down a recording of Acoustix singing So Long Mother or Irish Lullaby. (Then seek out Ambiance, an all-female group, doing their stunning *a cappella* Rhapsody in Blue.)(!!!!)

yeah yeah, in the use of sparse ambient passages and hushed transitional movements to bridge between rich material...

Many a tune during this Hampton run follows the same basic pattern:

1. **rock template** – AC/DC Bag's upcountry romp, dumbass party guitar in Mike's Song, Tweezer bashing away like a freshman losing his virginity, whatever Emotional Rescue is, endlessly Caucasian Ghost, Weekapaug to groove, someone's idea of fun aboard Halley's Comet[39] – reined in for...

2. **funky distillation** – all seven of those songs then ease off the gas, and Trey asserts some rhythm licks, usually with the ol' wah pedal in effect. The difference between this and the band's pre-1997 approach is Trey's refusal to start 'soloing,' settling into the rhythm bed instead, helping to construct the ensemble sound rather than dragging everyone behind him like a comet. Sometimes this movement gets into the pure 'cow funk' disco-nerd dance grooves everyone thinks of when they think of 1997 – slap bass, v against i in Trey's rhythm licks, a little tickle o' clavinet – but just as often it's a menacing funk-rock groove as in Mike's Song or Halley's, with Page staying on the piano and Trey moving between chord chops and melodic embellishments. (No solo statements here.) And there comes a feeling of...

---

[39] An ex-girlfriend once walked in on me listening to *The Soft Bulletin* – maybe the song Buggin', and noted that I don't place much importance on lyrics now do I. I choose to remember that she turned around, pleased with herself, and walked out smiling. I'm lucky she didn't walk in on Halley's Comet; I'd've been morally obligated to commit suicide right then and there. The song is that bad, that embarrassing.

3. **opening and expanse** – in the form of melancholy *dissipation* (Ghost), *distillation* (Tweezer, which goes nowhere and needs Black-Eyed Katy to come onboard to clear the air; Gumbo can go this way too), or *swell and crest* (Mike's Song, AC/DC Bag, and Halley's don't reach Phish's traditional rock 'peaks,' unusually, though they do top out and curl back). In the case of Halley's Comet, the band passes from its long funk build into a tense *mezzo forte* interlude spiked by angry percussion, and onto Trey's famous 'space jam' to close – for some this is a life-affirming musical moment. Hey I get ya. Meanwhile Mike's Song staggers through a fog, tensely pushing allways at once, to make it to its usual destination, Hydrogen. And at last it's…

4. **diminuendo and transition.** Ghost gets a closing sugarcoat and turns into Bag, which (after climactic procedural roar and twinkling hush comedown) moves quickly through a cross-rhythm exercise just to show we're all Very Serious; then it's Slave to change the subject. Halley's tumbles miles down from clouds of noise to a 'much-needed' dance tune, i.e. Tweezer, which in turn dies on the vine, seeding BEK. Emotional Rescue blows itself out and the boys get silly with the electronics for a couple minutes, then reassert that they're grown men by jumping into Split Open and Melt (spitting and snarling, 13 minutes plus).

The biggest deal is the fluidity of it all, its continuity: there are fewer styles on display in any one song (compared to the weaponized ironies of Phish's early/mid–90s stuff) but the music's intensity is amplified by the smooth (d)evolution and deformation between forms. And that was the point, or it was in part – wavelike movement, protean form, fractal growth.

You've gotta get at this music in the dark, I think. Phish's music is seasonal: after summer's carefree open air and spacious sound, Fall Tour brings out their claustrophilia, and they get to show off the knowledge they gained in the mid-90s of how to fill rooms like the Hampton Coliseum. Kuroda's lights are going the whole time: no stars, full dark. The touring crowds are a little different – the kids are stuck in school and anyone without a taste for cold weather is kept off the trail, so the intensity is ramped up a bit. It gets dark early indoors, the noise is doubled and redoubled by concrete walls, *time is lost*. The music comes out of that Weird environment and you gain something by reencountering it in the same context.

❤ ☞ ✽ ☞ ✳

Few musical moments generate the odd mix of melancholy, relief, and anticipation I get when Page starts the piano intro to Loving Cup. Phish have really made this song their own. Coming as it does on the heels of the dreamlike Ghost > Bag > Slave run on the 21st, the Stones closer at Hampton works to both run out the emotional thread and bring the set to a different *kind* of climax from the two that have already come (late in the Bag jam and at the end of Slave's long crescendo) (which is all Slave really is, really).

I saw a video once of Jack White sitting in with the Stones on Loving Cup. It was...terrible. The worst part, I realized, was that they didn't do the sensible thing and borrow back Phish's arrangement, which ends with the anthemic chords of 'what a beautiful buzz' instead of the stop-start movement of 'gimme a little drink.' The arrangement arrested the movement of the jam, or rather the endless guitar wanking – it was *incoherent* and I couldn't understand how a band known for its musical atmospherics could make such an elementary mistake of arrangement.

❤ ☞ ❋ ☞ ✳

Yesterday was 'neo-soul' day in our household, though the 'neo-' part of that term refers to a period 15 years gone[40] at this point: *Like Water for Chocolate, Mama's Gun, Things Fall Apart, Voodoo*. A specific sound and moment, its experimentalism masked somewhat by its (self-)conscious retrospective interest.

It's fascinating, not to mention humbling and slightly uncomfortable, to listen to Phish's late–90s live stuff against the incredible music coming from African-American groups at that time. I think of Phish as having attained something really pure and intense back then, which is true, sure, but the vocabulary I've always used to describe it – words like 'funk' and 'texture' and 'groove' and blather about 'protean form' and 'emotional openness' and blah blah – sounds a little *off* in the wake of something like 'Untitled (How Does It Feel)' off *Voodoo*. (This is so much about my own insecurities I admit but) I've always wanted to think that Phish had escaped their (our) (my) nerdy *whiteness* and found their (my) way into some shared Americo-erotic identity that would, uhh, I dunno get us all laid the all the ways I was hearing about in the glossy magazines.

But that didn't really happen; or rather something equally complicated and much less politely essentialist *did* happen, an extraordinary intensity *was* achieved, a new freedom of movement and elasticity of rhythm worked into the music and everyone listening was part of all those things. You still are, listening

---

[40] I'm old, I guess. Or lame? I'm certainly lame.

now (you're listening now, right?). The music can only be itself. So can we…

…although, now you mention it, the point of the music might after all be becoming-new(-something-or-other), which I think I've been trying to say all this time; *not that that's news* I hope; so maybe it's better to say we begin where we are, hold what we've brought and only that, and then we all have the chance to go together – parallel paths through private spaces within a wider shared space. *All at once.* That's the chance we're given **HEY LOOK I SOLVED RACISM** anyway so it's alright for Phish's 'funk' to be clumsy and ridiculous sometimes, or 'old-fashioned,' or even coolly machinic at one moment and (rhyme!) sweatily sentimental and anthemic the next, breaking out into some old familiar song. Or Bouncing Around the Room even.

Which was one of the first few Phish tunes I ever heard, come to think of it. Part of the template. Language learning. Unquestionably the *whitest fucking song ever written* too, which after the preceding couple of paragraphs I'm in no position to complain about and have no desire to apologize for.[41]

Hey by the way is everyone cool with me solving racism, by the way?

♥ ☞ ♣ ☞ ✳

A quick note on the Hampton Soundcheck Jam included in the Hampton/NC box set: it contains some of the most compelling music of the tour. (There's also a lot of dicking around.) Before it begins to wander, the jam previews the brokedown sonics of What's the Use? for 10ish minutes while avoiding any resolution or catharsis.

I've come to value improvisations that go someplace interest-

---

[41] Though then again I did mention it. And mention (here) mentioning it.

ing, dwell there awhile, explore, and never tip over into a musical 'answer' or settlement. Phish's music tends to have a strong narrative arc (usually 'start low, go slow; get higher, catch on fire') and their greatest-I-think jams do reach powerful climaxes, the 11/22 Halley's among them, but one of the remarkable qualities of Fall 97 is the way the music kept moving and shifting without losing coherence *or* going for the ready-made Climactic Major Chord Roar every time. Sometimes the results were boring – the Emotional Rescue that opens the 11/21 show, for instance – but the band kept finding ways to *grow* from one musical segment to another rather than forcing the issue with an all-at-once key change or unmotivated accelerando or convenient segue.

The Hampton shows are best known for their climactic tunes (AC/DC Bag, Halley's, Hood, Rescue > Split, etc.) but they also suggest the natural endpoint of Phish's experiments in funk-flavoured minimalism: hushed introspection and enveloping atmospheres rather than virtuosic ostentation. This dynamic playing was always leading, ironically, toward the sound of *static*.

NOVEMBER 23, WINSTON-SALEM

I: My Soul, Theme > BEK, Sparkle, Twist > Stash > NICU, Fluffhead > Char0 **II:** Gin > Disease > Low Rider > Disease, Bold As Love **E:** Julius

The flip side of the Hampton shows, maybe the best argument for the canonical status of Fall 97. Something dark and dangerous was in the air. Very little funk, but what's here is Phish's best performance of Black-Eyed Katy, a *sublime* piece of work (Trey's less the soloist than the conductor; the climax is supernatural). Instead of James Brown, Hendrix is boss here. The second set starts with 40 minutes of primal scream therapy and only then surrenders to the band's indomitably sunny disposition (with a silly Low Rider 'cover' and triumphant return to Down with Disease). The Stash > NICU diptych is a hidden bonus, escaping from a frightening (but danceable!) Stash jam by way of a heroic segue.

Just an extraordinary night of music. I've listened to it a lot since the box set was released, but only a fraction of the amount of time I've spent with the Hampton shows, especially 11/22. Here's something 'funny': my esteem for each of the three shows, which fit perfectly together despite their differences, is inversely proportional to the frequency with which I listen to them. This is arguably the 'best' of the three in some ways, and inarguably my least favourite.[42]

♥ ☞ ♣ ☞ ✵

One thing about playing *long* songs live, 'jamming' in other words, is that the nature of the show, the overall vibe of the experience, can be dramatically altered by a single tune – the hard-edged funk of the December 6 Tweezer gives way to that intergalactic 3/4 jam and the night turns into something new, or *here* the lights fade out slowly on Twist and Stash becomes a kind of continuation – tiptoe funk and maddening minor-key Latinism blend into a creepy creatures-at-play movement, all fuzz-drone underpinning and fluorescent synth slides and Fishman's spry tom-tom work to count off the seconds before the fucking bomb goes off…

---

[42] If this were a different kind of essay – which maybe it will be later, who can tell – this would be the place to talk about how we (choose to) remember past loves, why so many people hold it against others when they feel vulnerable, as if love had to be pulled from within the spoiled body like oil from the ground. But nope.

...which it does later on, as you'd hope, in the form of Gin and everything after. There are distinct movements to this concert as a whole: a blues warmup, then grand melodrama in Theme and Katy and a quick Sparkle interlude to up the tempo. Then into the dark: Twist > Stash, and NICU to dispel some tension. Finally the raucous set closers: Fluffhead, a journey in itself, and the obligatory Character Zero to finish. But damn, the prevailing darkness: and Gin, which was designed as a happy-go-lucky up jam,[43] doozles along for about 13 minutes before souring permanently in the heat of Trey's, um, guitar freak-out(?!).

Honestly, after that Twist/Stash combo I'd've been annoyed if they *hadn't* followed the rabbit down down down to see what the dark had to say. This Gin is the message they brought back.

♥ ☞ ♣ ☞ ✳

(from 'There is a shiny brass lamp nearby,' summer 2010)

a single stone weighing twenty-five pounds. imagine the terror, yes, but then the anger: this damned thing will kill me by inches, ounces. by hours. this stupidity will be the death of me. think of how lonely that would feel, what questions might run through your head in those last hours. this is my fault. rookie mistake. i was never half the man they raised me to be. my name on one cave but i end up in this one. well what better place to die. but never to see stars again, my wife, my daddy – do they get on without me? how? the devil's in the stone. a passage further down. he crept out of a hole in the earth when i wasn't looking, put out my lamplight, and put this stone in my path where i could knock it down. gave me this mistake to make, to take. and i took it.

---

[43](and is, yet again, in all seriousness, one of the worst songs ever written. It's like Reba's slow cousin with worse grades at school)

goddamn fool. stupid and weak and i deserve it. no. please don't let me end up like this inside the stone. in this hole in the ground. this is a grave. ha, my cave. is a. oh god. i'm in hell. another fifty, sixty feet down and there's a doorway marked hell, and when i wasn't looking the devil opened it up and put out my light, and crept back down into hell on feet like limewater, just slipping across the rocks. he doesn't even touch the walls. he's the cold air. he slips across the rock. my face, he touches my face. i feel his fingertips. cold air. whatever's down there whispers. no that rustling is my hand, i had it up in front of me, i didn't know. broke my leg my back and broke me, the devil did. my fault. i am an accident. i put that stone up there so it would – brought it down on my own self. the roof. wait. that sound is please i can hear it it's my wife she's saying come back to me baby come back floyd –

I think of (talk about a country of the imagination!) Phish's Fall 1997 stuff as dark, Weird even; and in writing about it I tend to use metaphorical descriptors like 'subterranean' or 'ocean-floor'(?). That's the feeling the music gives me, so much of the time: the doors close on the amphitheatre, lights down, and the space begins to fill up with cold water, purple and blue light filtering sickly through, horrible creatures swimming by darklit from within, a rumble beneath the ocean floor makes the mountains shimmer and begin slowly to fall…

This isn't quite that – there's too much sprint-to-nothing guitar madness to get deep and dark – but listening to my audience recording of the show after spending much time with the (soundboard) box set, I'm struck again by the way Trey's heavily compressed guitar seems to *surround* the audience instead of attacking directly. Just the sound of it, never mind the actual 'making of notes.' There's none of the slashing, aggressive lead sound you associate with hard rock guitar, nor again the clean round tone of jazz guitar. Trey's Fall 97 guitar sound is like a principle of immersion. I can't even describe it – I hear his pick scraping the string, then there's this almost human tone in the next instant, thin and round like words spoken through a drinking straw.

Thing is, the *whole band* sounds like that – or rather, they all add up to a sound that has the same enfolding quality. They're playing to the room, *with* its contours and contents, and the lack of clarity is a deliberate stylistic choice. Mike is more audible than ever before,[44] but between Trey's sound, Fish's feathery snare work, and Page's ongoing clav affair (has anyone ever gotten as horny for clavinet as Page McConnell in 1997?) they're like…a Potemkin band: barely even three-dimensional.

But it's a great sound all the same, perfect for the cold-ass funkspace they were trading in back in the days before the millennial turnover had done its monumentally disappointed civilizational *plop plop fizz fizz*. Perfect too for headphonic descent and seafloor touchdown on the, what, the couch? the fucking *futon?* after toddler and beloved wife go to sleep. Probably I've learned to read *into* the sound as hazy aquatic twilight rather than actually heard the latter in the former. Fallacies of causation and the blah blah. Still, I love the sound, which sounds like…a band that sounds like 'Fish.' The right voice for saying what it's saying, is what I'm saying.

Ever notice how 'sink or swim' is a false choice?

---

[44] The evolution of Mike's 5-string guitar sound over the years is worthy of its own article. Right now, in 2012, he's developed a flexible lead bass voice that – coupled with his judicious use of filters and FX – lets him turn on a dime from nimble upper-register melodic leads to floor-shaking synth bombs to underwater gurgle-slaps to that rubbery dance-dweeb Boogie On sound. Leading his own band has made a huge difference to Mike's musicianship and his technical approach. I love the way he's playing these days.

♥ ☞ ✣ ☞ ✳

Listening to the 6/23/00 Gin again. Trey's looping his bright trills over a midtempo two-chord climax that seems to go on for ages. To jog my memory I follow it up with the famous Went Gin (8/17/97), which is *awwwwwwwwwfully similar* but with that added vi chord for unexpected melancholy melodrama. Then the wonderfully inventive 11/9/98 Gin, the 11/19/97 Champaign version with its cheeky segue into Llama, and finally back to Winston-Salem to realize that *this* Gin went off to thrashville partly because (for whatever reason) it didn't, maybe just couldn't, cohere into the usual Gin-jam form. Because I know where the jam is going, I can hear the slow repetitive section around the 13:00 mark as *prologue* to the heavy stuff to come; but I think there's something uncomfortable going on there: like the Wolfman's from Champaign (11/19), this improvisation can't quite find its usual colours and falls into mannerism for a bit, then Trey sends it shooting off into an equally uncomfortable but more generative space.

At Coventry, Phish's final festival before the breakup in 2004, Trey gave a speech after a mournful Velvet Sea (with an unusually aggressive guitar solo as I recall). Unsurprisingly, Trey broke down during the speech. Then he gathered himself and made this announcement.

> And what we need to do right now is just…blow off some fucking steam for the rest of the night, because…
>
> I keep looking at the *clock*…

As you'd expect, the crowd ate up the first part; the band members almost never swear onstage, and it's rare to hear a musician say 'We are doing it wrong, we need something new here.'

But that last line…it terrifies me. When I listen to the speech, the hairs on the back of my neck stand up.

He sounds so scared.

The band launched, then, into a half-hour Split Open and Melt, which provided the exorcism they sorely needed, particularly during a monstrous seven-minute ambient coda[45] that's some of the darkest abstract music Phish has ever played. That long Split jam is something like the 11/23 Gin and 11/19 Wolfman's freakouts: a counterspell to stave off lethargy. It's nice to think that the angrier Fall 97 jams are a birthing process by which new levels of emotional intensity and presence are achieved and slowly acclimated to…the alternative, that Trey is a really impatient individual prone to fits of Follow the Leader aggression, is less appealing – and it can't explain the Coventry Velvet Sea anyway.

I like a nice Story.

❤ ☞ ♣ ☞ ✻

The music becomes the calendar.

They say that at millennial moments, true believers cease to live in 'normal time,' and instead occupy (and drag others into) 'apocalyptic time,' the cognitive-literal *end times* within which people, events, ideas, and identities are yoked to a destiny-

---

[45] I like to think of the black-ambient Coventry Split coda as the horrible offspring or diseased continuation of two long jams from IT: the grotesquely beautiful Waves outro and the terminal 46 Days jam. The latter stretches 40 minutes into the darkest part of night and is either one of Phish's most extraordinary live statements or something like a death knell; or both and surely more. Though honestly it's more like the same weekend's Spread It Round jam than anything else – but I don't particularly *enjoy* that jam, for whatever reason (maybe because I know they play Bug right after?) so I choose to believe otherwise. 'Wally, you're a bad person.' Yeah I know. Oh by the way, did you notice the very very brief Vultures tease in the outro of the IT Disease?

narrative. At such moments you can justify anything in terms of a ready-made moral frameup. Time's running out in a real, physical sense. Spacetime warps around the narrative skeleton.

I'm sorry to say I think of late–90s American culture in terms of a coarsely millennial story. The events of September 2001 make that easy, in retrospect, and I can't separate my historical understanding of *that* apocalyptic moment from personal concerns: love and death survived, family lost found and newly made, comfortable identity worn away.

Some days I miss the strange paranoid/pronoid air of those days. The Internet was gonna link up every living human and every functioning machine, and all would join and be joined in a nationless digital state; but Big Brother would come in the door with everyone else. Something called 'globalization' blah blah; and Hitchens said it sounded like a nice idea, an internationalist idea – *solidarity* after all. Giant amounts of money were being made and lost by engineers, of all creatures. The ozone something something. The New Age. I went to a store called *Bell Book and Candle* in San Juan with a girl named Margarita and bought a tarot deck, and it took me 15 years to look at it. I read this...

> To choose order over disorder, or disorder over order, is to accept a trip composed of both the creative and the destructive. But to choose the creative over the destructive is an all-creative trip composed of both order and disorder.

...in the *Principia* but didn't get it, couldn't wouldn't will not no, and kept on missing its wisdom for the same 15 years.

I spent half the wages from my first summer job in college on Miles and Trane. All those orange LP sleeves from Impulse! on my shelves. I'd go to sleep listening to *A Love Supreme* and dry off after a shower standing on the roof of our home naked singing whatever songs I could remember. I got scared of Y2K (I blame *Wired* magazine) and scared my little brother in turn. He's never forgiven me.

One November Phish played a show in North Carolina and ghosts rose up out of the floor to eat everyone whole. Drank down coloured light and in dark they got to killing the young people first who might otherwise have run.

A week later I went to my one show of tour, in Worcester. The black cold sea floor where dragons sleep. I was wholly there and theirs.

Couple years later there was a show in the Everglades and I hardly even knew it was happening. Some several ten thousands in a swamp all night just dancing. Purgation.

You measure the *years* by it. By the new minds you think into.

We listened to *Kind of Blue* in the morning and she wore always nothing under her Navy uniform and was surprised how much she trusted me.

He was dead for days before I found out at the piano the morning I turned twenty-one, and I kept playing awhile before I could begin to know what I'd heard.

I flew in just in time to listen to a machine breathe for her. Dead of night she fell away and we got a phone call.

Or just singing with *The Joshua Tree* up the mountains on the second day of our drive in matching purple flightsuits and each a different silly nametape; mine wasn't even fully sewn on, I was so *lazy*. Before Des Moines and those two friendly girls at the gas station or Chicago at what's-her-name's house each of us squeezed between the bed and the wall, 'Canyonlands style' the term was; but no I was on the bed instead, ha ha ha.

Or holding Emily's hand under the Great Dome watching people die by the thousands on TV on a Tuesday and Phish had broken up just a year prior and so who do you turn to? When tears aren't enough I mean.

I wrote and said and thought and wanted horrible things and my world was much much too small.

The music becomes the time. I can't even see my own area code (617) without thinking of 17 June 1994.

I wasn't there. Hell I feel like I wasn't really alive then, how could I have been? I didn't know a river ran beneath where I stood. Apocalyptic time. Mirror time.

Someone has arrived at the library now wearing a black hat like a comic-book Australian. I believe she's daft; it's not the hat makes me say so. I have to go. Pick up my son and wife, my very existence. Steal time back from mere Event. Move the story forward.

(LET'S LET THE MASTER HANDLE THIS NEXT BIT)

> Lovers of global conspiracy, not all of them Catholic, can count on the Masons for a few good shivers and voids when all else fails. One of the best of the classic Weird Mason Stories has Doctor Livingstone (living stone? oh, yes) come wandering into a native village in, not even the heart, but the subconscious of Darkest Africa, a place, a tribe he's never seen before: fires in the silence, unfathomable stares, Livingstone ambles up to the village chief and flashes him a Masonic high sign – the chief recognizes it, returns it, all smiles, and orders every fraternal hospitality laid on for the white stranger. But recall that Dr. Livingstone, like Wernher von Braun, was born close to the Spring Equinox, and so had to confront the world from that most singular of the Zodiac's singular

points.... Well, and keep in mind where those Masonic Mysteries came from in the first place. [...]

[T]he Masons had long, long degenerated into just another businessmen's club. A real shame. Business of all kinds, over the centuries, had atrophied certain sense-receptors and areas of the human brain, so that for most of the fellows taking part, the present-day rituals were no more, and even maybe a little less, than hollow mummery. Not for all of them, though. Now and then you found a throwback. [...]

The magic in these Masonic rituals is very, very old. And way back in those days, it worked. As time went on, and it started being used for spectacle, to consolidate what were only secular appearances of power, it began to lose its zip. But the words, moves, and machinery have been more or less faithfully carried down over the millennia, through the grim rationalizing of the World, and so the magic is still there, though latent, needing only to touch the right sensitive head to reassert itself. (Thomas Pynchon, *Gravity's Rainbow*)

NOVEMBER 26, HARTFORD

I: Tweezer > Sparkle > Gumbo > My Soul, McGrupp, Dirt, Melt, Horse > Silent, Taste **II:** Char0 > 2001 > Cities > Ya Mar > Punch > Caspian, Poor Heart > Tweeprise **E:** Cavern

Interesting temporal logic to the show. First set alternates between long tunes (Tweezer 18min, Gumbo 12min, McGrupp 10min, Taste 12min to close) and brief interregna (Sparkle 4min, My Soul 7min, Dirt 4min, HorseSilent 7min). Rough work of keeping up a first set flow – conscious imposition. 'Variety' of genre, a palette-cleanser after each large course. The second set, though, goes 21min, 14min, 8min, 7min, 8min, 11min, 2min, 3min. Minor fall, major lift, then sharp exhalation to close. Brief encore, out.

Falling into a dream and climbing back out to find morning waiting.

Here's a nice little Tweezer, by the way, which serves the standard Fall Tour show-opener function of getting the audience moving free and easy while tightening up the band. Ears and eyes together. Long, patient build, quite Katy-like – nothing Phish can't do in their sleep even now, but the effortlessness of the Tweezer isn't exactly a mark against it. And a wonderfully primary-coloured jam for when the hard funking's done.

Interesting that they go right back to that well after a short break – sludgy Tweezer, doofy Sparkle raveup, then a sinister dance jam in Gumbo (upping tempo as it goes, to a predatory lope by track's end) to announce the night's overall mood. The funk jams do important *work* for the band in these shows: musical-machinic computation, figuring out the angles, freeing up their human resources. Leave the formal complication to the robot servitors and let the people dance.

Makes sense that Trey'd swerve from that jams's final movement, angry anthem, to an up blues. Wave away the smoke. Blues is old and we're deep inside the earth after all. It comes from here. Zion.

♥ ☞ ♣ ☞ ✽

The very ending's kind of a joke actually – an unexpected, totally out-of-place return to the singsong goofiness of the first set, sticking a superfluous Poor Heart (two minutes of bluegrass comedy) between the towering 70-minute second set jam, with its magnificent Caspian closer, and the necessary catharsis of Tweezer Reprise. Impressively, this classic set has all the variety of the first set, but it still flows as well as any other Fall 97 performance – 2001 and Cities are both funk workouts, but different enough in mood that the band has to step lightly to make the transition work, and the rest of the tunes in the second frame occupy wholly distinct genres. Zero's a heavy set-closing guitar stomp; 2001 is quickstep galactic dance-funk; Phish's take on Talking Heads' Cities slows David Byrne's nervy afroweird beat down to a late-nite plod; Ya Mar's a spirited calypso dweebfest; Punch blends rock swagger and Latin stagger before a squealing noise outro; Caspian's pure nerd-church anthem; Poor Heart and Tweeprise as above. It's a real genre catalogue, impressive given the sometime monochromaticism of the tour's jamming style…

…but it *works* is the thing, they manage to combine every element of their musical identity right then into a continuous suite that's its own whole big thing. It's the kind of musical performance you dream of putting on, or even just seeing live – a Night Unto Itself. Trey keeps the proceedings moving smoothly at every step, finding a comfortable midpoint between his bandleader and psych-voyager identities. The sweeping full-band climax of Caspian pays off the whole show, releasing all the potential energy built up by unfinished versions of Zero, 2001, Ya Mar, even Tweezer's roundtopped anticlimax and the sharp move to cut off Gumbo. It all builds to that five-minute stretch in Caspian, waves of sound receding…even the way *in* to Caspian has a valedictory feel, with nearly two minutes of hushed full-band interplay before Trey's annunciatory guitar strokes and that perfect opening lyric.[46]

It's no surprise that a consistently free, fluid approach to im-

---

[46]Shame about the rest of the words though. 'Oh, to be Prince Caspian afloat upon the waves' is a resonant image on its own and the bedraggled courage and resignation of the music can move you, but 'stumps instead of feet'? 'Demons in their caves'? I like *Dungeons & Dragons* way more than the next guy but that shit's too much.

provisatory movement produces consistently dream-logical flow (whatever the manifest content of the music itself, the genre grab-bag). I think maybe it's the movement logic rather than any particular harmonic blah blah that determines our overall emotional response; harmony and rhythm and melody are tactical choices, implementations, but first and last there's a choice of language, the frame itself shifts, the matrix; and all (musical, human) objects caught within are translated at once…

In any case it's a fantastic show. There's nothing bad to say about it, really. So why say more? The main event is Character Zero, which runs twice its typical length and never quite arrives at a climax, setting the scene for a half-hour danceathon before Caspian clears the smoke. If you like Phish at all then you have to hear this show. Blistering Taste to close the first set too.

So what?

> I like to compare evolution to weaving of a great tapestry. The strong unyielding warp of this tapestry is formed by the essential nature of elementary non- living matter, and the way in which this matter has been brought together in the evolution of our planet. In building this warp the second law of thermodynamics has played a predominant role. The multi-colored woof which forms the detail of the tapestry I like to think of a having been woven onto the warp principally by mutation and natural selection. While the warp establishes the dimensions and supports the whole, it is the woof that most intrigues the aesthetic sense of the student of organic evolution, showing as it does the beauty and variety of fitness of organisms to their environment. But why should we pay so little attention to the warp, which is after all a basic part of the whole structure? Perhaps the analogy would be more complete if something were introduced that is occasionally seen in textiles – the active participation of the warp

> in the pattern itself. Only then, I think, does one grasp the full significance of the analogy. (Harold Blum, 1968)

Think of this music as a reduction or distillation of an immensely complicated form which had undergone a kind of fractal development from a simple seed – a macroorganism undergoing collapse after passing a critical point of maximum sustainable population, maybe, or the meringue falling in on itself (is that something that happens to meringue?) and turning into, I dunno, a funky pancake. Studded with stars! This metaphor is *fucked,* sorry, just stay with me: Phish's music got so damned busy in the early 1990s that they had to move in a whole different direction, we've been through this, and this move triggered a catastrophic cascade that stripped away its surface complication, leaving only the endoskeleton, the Big Idea, 'which is…communication.'[47]

All the formal features of the old music are here, but the rough edges are filed off, and the internal organization is stronger, cleaner, more consistent, more coherent. More welcoming too. Each song takes you somewhere, and the next tune picks you up at that same spot – no antagonistic imposition from a perverse setlist writer. Just a growing feeling of inevitability. Complex figures self-organize locally and collapse, their materials freely redistributed throughout the field.

This is optimism, or (a much better word I think) *faith.* Total trust in other human beings is stupid and wise. It's necessary. It's

---

[47] If you haven't watched *Specimens of Beauty,* the little documentary that came with the *Undermind* CD, do track it down. The interview with a manic, runny-nosed Trey is both dark foreshadowing of the band's breakup and a glimpse of a nervy genius finding again his bliss among friends – when he talks about the many ideas they've started to let go of, leaving room for the 'biggest idea of all,' he seems to be made of light. Longtime fans of the band feel a personal connection to the musicians, Trey especially, and that moment makes me feel like a friend has seen a god.

essential.

Finally they were them.

That's what I'm hearing here. Not 'great jams' though yeah those too...what I'm/we're hearing is four men testifying through their art to their faith in one another, which is to say, *in the shared moment.*

Yes! Yes that's actually it. Yes you can *too* hear it.

Kids know when they're being lied to. Adults seem to welcome deception, weirdly, foolishly – but you never lose that skill, you just stop trusting it. Filtering out the signal your senses send you. But lights go down and the noise picks up and you choose (or don't) to trust your sisters and brothers. Even the four guys onstage.

Phish fans are trusting sorts, or aspire to be. Oh sidebar by the way: that's why it's so fun and easy to *steal their shit.*

NOVEMBER 28–30, WORCESTER

I: Curtain > YEM > I Didn't Know, Maze, Farmhouse, Katy, Theme > Rocky Top **II:** Timber, Limb, Slave > Ghost > Johnny B Good **E:** My Soul

I: Wedge, Foam, Simple > Yesterday > Avenu Malkenu > Yesterday, Sloth, Ginseng, Saw It Again, Horn, Water, Bowie **II:** Jim > Design > Hood > Caspian, Suzy **E:** Buffalo Bill, Moby Dick > Fire

I: Guyute, Bitch, Wolfman's > Love Me, Coil, Loving Cup **II:** NICU, Stash > Free > Jam > Piper > Circus, Antelope **E:** Them Changes

There's a wonderful book called *A General Theory of Love* which posits that 'love' is a kind of communication protocol, an emotional Morse code (or TCP/IP!). The theory goes something like this: in order to fit their huge brains through the birth canal, humans are born before their bodies/brains are fully ready for the world – hence the unusual vulnerability of human newborns and infants (an infant horse can run from a predator; humans take years to reach that point). As Harvey Karp puts it, the first three months of human life are a 'fourth trimester' during which the baby's more like a fetus than a toddler.

To make up for infant vulnerability, humans (indeed, all mammals) are able to affect one another's emotions, and indeed biorhythms of all kinds – from heartbeat to sleep patterns to speech patterns to respiratory habits – through physical contact and proximity. Babies breathe more steadily, and their hearts beat more predictably, when their mothers hold them close; their bodily systems *mimic nearby rhythms.* Babies learn how to feel, how to time and regulate responses, from those around them (even from nonhumans, which is why dogs are such great childhood companions).

The *General Theory* refers to these subconscious communications as limbic resonance (sharing), limbic regulation (stabilizing), and limbic revision (learning).

If you've ever wondered why so many moms instinctively bounce their babies at 80rpm, consider a typical resting heartrate, and how you might teach a child's heart to keep landing square on the downbeat…

…and then listen to the 11/28 YEM and Ghost, nice long versions (YEM is 24 minutes without a vocal jam) which come second and second-last in the show, respectively, and which feature more or less identical cow-funk jams – snazziest of the year by some counts. Throughout the year Phish started shows with rockers and funk numbers, to limber up the fingers and bring minds into alignment (*minds are things bodies do*); here they come back to their doofy cargo-cult funk language as an organizing principle in the show's climactic spot, switching YEM and Ghost's customary slots and letting the dweebadelic disc-oh ball keep spinning as an *end in itself*. The rhythm has *intrinsic* value.

That YEM resonates. Ghost regulates. And to stay with the whole tour, to learn those lights and goof-groove moves down deep in your bones, to learn new ways of being and listening, spaces reorganizing how you think of space, well...

Damn, they even go to Slave in the #3 slot, second frame, and *then* pull up into a dance-freakout to close. (I don't even have the Johnny B Goode on my hard drive; this may seem weird, but I *hate* that song, so I made a 30-second mp3 that fades out before they can get into it. So yeah, they actually close the show with old-fashioned rock-raveup stuff. But there's nothing to it, really.)

It's worlds away from the Hampton shows, though, which are even heavier on a plodding swamp-funk vibe – Tweezer instead of Ghost, Mike's instead of YEM, that interminable Emotional Rescue (what a title!) – and which climax in that wild Halley's 'space jam' instead of, well, what happens on the 29th and 30th in Worcester.

I say it's all part of a continuous arc: some dark Event in the midwest, icy depths in Hampton, hellfire in Winston-Salem, continued exorcism in Hartford, then on to their home turf in Danceachusetts for three nights in a different register. (And Thanksgiving inbetween, of course.) Much as the Hartford show keeps to a continuous emotional contour, giving coherence to its varied second set, the whole tour seems to move smoothly between shows that (if only in retrospect) seem to be conceived holistically, as part of a greater narrative. Even though I know that's *not* the case – the band worked without setlists and began each show without preconceptions about the course of the evening – that narrative throughline, my own interpretive imposition, is part of the deep pleasure these shows give me.

And yeah, I do believe I'm responding to some emotional logic present in the shows themselves; the contour becomes apparent not from poring over setlists but from listening to the music, the Thing Itself. You've got no choice, really. You gotta go back to the world.

11/28 isn't much of a show in the grand scheme of things but in the context of this tour it hits *hard*.

And it's the 'weakest' of the three nights, the only one that doesn't contain at least one all-time classic something or other!

Love is one means by which human emotional computation is *parallelized*. You might say we're naturally funk-minimalists who just…forget.

These Worcester shows are about getting (it) together.

♥ ☞ ♣ ☞ ✻

Remember this maneuver: 10ish minutes into Simple on the 29th, midway through a fine jukebox set, they lightly step from that song's I-I7-IV-V outro jam to a tensely beautiful IV. This reduces the informational load, so to speak, and ironically this resolution sets up a lingering longing to return to the I, which makes the intrinsically satisfying I7-IV movement complexly *un*satisfying for a moment; but you settle into it and it becomes the new harmonic homebase, and that's the song's final minute. Hanging on the IV chord is a useful trick to change the feel of a jam without forcing the music from its well-worn track: jamdweebs, *know that*.

Then Trey starts those chiming arpeggios signaling that the title tune of his rock opera, *The Man Who Stepped into Yester-*

day, is beginning – but he's doing two mildly disconcerting but generative things at that moment:

1. playing these beautiful chords a tritone away from what Mike and Page are doing, which is a powerful ear-tingling dissonance; and

2. playing TMWSIY in the *wrong key anyway,* starting up the reprise instead of the opening, so after this startling, lovely transition he then gets to head three frets north – a minor third modulation – which (in an almost pedantically literal way, sorry) makes for an even more *elevating* musical moment.

There's no break in the music's flow, is the thing. (God, I could listen to this song forever.) The music ebbs and flows, gently breathing into a full-band climax, and Trey's weirdly upbeat arrangement of Avenu Malkenu (not exactly the cheery crackling hearth of Hebrew litanies) kicks in. When I describe it in words, Trey's brief key-changing adventure seems like a very small mistake that proceeds, by welcoming dream-logic, to open up a new musical space for the players. Yay accessible, generative polytonality!

I'd pay a similar compliment, with similar asterisks and footnotes, to the famous second-set Runaway Jim from the same night. By the 12-minute mark the band is bursting the song's seams, and two minutes later they're into a completely new space thanks to Fishman's hard brake and everyone else's ominous atmospheric playing; but this sizable musical step is made confidently and *fluidly,* carrying the energy of the frenetic Jim jam into a slackerbeat interlude.

I don't actually *like* this prefatory lameass pseudoblues slow jam – the whole hourlong Jim Symphony is strongly reminiscent of Phish's 1994–95 genre-catalogue psych-outs but with a smoother logic and more patience, and/but *this* segment reminds me uncomfortably of their stupid joke-blues affectations, e.g. in the May 1994 Bomb Factory Tweezer – but even when Trey grows audibly tired of the bullshit, the band is unwilling to damage the delicate tissue of the moment. The jam's next segment layers Trey's busy 'space jam' guitar style over a full-bodied rock groove, which effectively blows away any cobwebs and clears the way for some crabwalking dissonance of an old sort with a new sound – wah-funk rhythm guitar instead of confrontational mini-phrases, atmospheric rolling bass, heady textures alternately leaving and filling space...it's all very much a single long-form piece, an honest (hourlong) moment. Some of it's drearily familiar, or just dreary, but the uniquely that-moment-then-and-only-that bit is the way the atmosphere settles in slowly rather than being slapped on top of the audience by the onstage musical director.

This is what democracy sounds like.

But then of course in one of life's charming little ironies the best-loved part of this whole show, the Weekapaug Jam, is pretty much the one stretch of music to emerge purely from Trey's stubborn insistence on his Neat Idea – maybe the *least* democratic moment of the show. Not that it matters, nice is nice, but I wouldn't wanna let that slide by without comment. The intensity of the preceding 50ish minutes is brought to a head, deepened and crazified and cork-popped, by the *bandleader.* So much for utopian idealism![48]

---

[48]For what it's worth, I prefer the similarly extended 8/11/98 Jim, which has a lot in common with the Worcester behemoth but (1) actually closes with the Jim lyrics after 34 minutes and one 'Moon River' tease despite (2) never really climaxing at all, which (3) makes for kind of a weird overall experience, (4) but still lovely. Hell, I think I prefer (today) the somewhat laborious 8/

❤ ☞ ♣ ☞ ✱

Having listened to this music for so long – obsessively for the second half of the 90s, regularly throughout the 2000s, and a hell of a lot since the band got back together in 2009 – I find that I can't *integrate* my Phish listening with other music. I'm not sure what produces this dynamic – defensiveness? possessiveness? overfamiliarity? It could be embarrassment, of course; I'm not above that.

Listening now to the 11/28 Ghost – a very strong performance with a blaring (instead of slyly funking) stop/start middle section – I'm trying to imagine adding this to a playlist. It's too precise and rhythmically square to sit easily among jazz tracks (I cued up some Masabumi Kikuchi earlier and felt like I was eavesdropping on cafe chat in a foreign country – my ear had forgotten how to dig Kikuchi's (awesome) rhythmic/harmonic language), and both too fastidious and too dorky-dreamy-dancey to make perfect sense in a rock mix. It's a swell jam on its own terms but the terms are all its own.

I mean, you throw on *Funk Power 1970: A Brand New Thang* or *Hell* and yeah, it's clear Phish ganked *some* of the Godfather's rhythm thing (Fishman's ability to absorb drum styles is one of Phish's secret weapons), but you can't help noticing how Phish's usual thing is to *unwind* a funk groove, to increase the tonal density while kinda smoothing out the rhythmic complexity (even in the 97-era pure uncut funk-for-its-own-sake stuff). But Jesus Christ, how do you fit even the *nastiest* Ghost jam into a mix with James Brown? Or Funkadelic, another of Phish's obvious late-career touchstones, who could keep these machinic

---

31/12 Dick's Jim, which for various reasons *needed* to be 20 minutes long and shows it, but which happily maintains the manic party vibe of that whole weekend.

rhythms going for ten minutes and alter the sound and shape of the music by *deepening* the groove rather than altering its form, while (by the sound of it) everyone who's not hammering out this unbelievable funk groove is fucking like a freak up top of the speakers or hanging from the ceiling on a like purple velvet sex couch?[49]

Phish can get heavy and deep while improvising but *usually* they don't, or they don't stay that way; high and light is the aim most nights, it feels like. I'm spinning the epic Worcester version of Funky Bitch right now, with the face-melting climax to Trey's guitar solo around 4:20 or so, the entire band peaking *effortlessly* and making a decent case for 'yes we can play blues and funk without it seeming like comedy or a tribute to "the real thing,"' and as much as I love this tune and coherent[50] fine-point musical climaxes in general, when I randomly choose an album from my Pile of Musical Absolutely Yes – *What's Going On* this time – I hear deeper funk and more intense melancholy but almost no increase in volume through the whole album.

In fact the songs on that album seem to get quieter over time, backing off to make room for new sounds that heighten the experience without assaulting the senses. Check out how the echoing percussion hits on Mercy Mercy Me blend seamlessly into the choral vocals in the song's final minute. Or how Right On starts out with funky piano/snare and percussive flute playing but reaches its emotional peak after the drum kit drops out,

---

[49] I lived for four years in a house with a three-abreast carseat suspended on chains from the ceiling of a second-floor room that saw more orgies than, for instance, *your* bedroom I'm betting, or mine for that matter; and I breathed in many a fine evening listening to what in those days passed for drugpop among a certain brand of hardcore-forebrain geek, i.e. IDM I guess you'd call it. Folks who'd just discovered *Dark Side of the Moon* and hadn't yet heard it sober, to notice how goddamn boring, how offensively *easy* that album is. I should've been studying but many days I don't regret, y'know, not.

[50] (as in lasers, or the final bars of What You Want)

leaving strings, handheld percussion, glockenspiel, sax, quiet piano, and other 'soft' elements – the rhythmic pulse continues as the harmonies slowly descend, naturally quieting, building tension, so that the return of the backbeat is climactic release even though it's only a *touch* faster and louder than the opening.

I know Phish can do this; that's not the question. But it's not just about this (very fine) take on Ghost – listening to the Timber jam from the top of the 2nd set on the 28th, I feel the same weird linguistic isolation. Shit, is it just me? (Would I be better off writing about something else, for my hearing's sake?) Or am I having a hard time integrating this music into existing categories because Phish really do present a strangely self-contained musical world, borrowing sonic/formal terms from existing musics without ever slotting neatly into anyone else's generic scheme?

I mean for heaven's sake their best 'Latin' tune is TASTE, which if you've heard the song you'll understand why the word 'Latin' is in quotes but hopefully it's clear too where the rhythmic ideas in that song come from, even if the harmonies sound like something from Raymond Scott…

♥ ☞ ♣ ☞ ✻

While (at first) listening to the 11/30 Stash:

I find joy, these last few years, in a particular cognitive oscillation that you may recognize. When I'm reading a story I first experience its formal elements as familiar ('oh that's just a Wild West *X-Men*,' 'oh this is pulp Nazis vs the Cthulhu Mythos') and have trouble reading away from those intertextual connections. After a while I sink into the story (Tony Soprano stops being 'Ralph Kramden in *Goodfellas*' and achieves imaginative autonomy) and experience the bliss of fictional immersion; but at some point I become conscious of the story fitting into a new imaginative matrix, which isn't about texts at all but rather about *worlds*.

I (choose to) read Pynchon's *The Crying of Lot 49*, Delany's *Dhalgren*, Mark Danielewski's *Only Revolutions*, and Belize's heavenly vision in Tony Kushner's *Angels in America* as having a shared *setting* or mythic space – and Belize's city, an angelic San Francisco, is both the Jerusalem of the *Song of Songs* and the spiritual/sexual utopia described in the following lyric:

> There will be a new city with streets of gold
> Young so educated they never grow old
> There will be no death
> For with every breath
> A voice of many colours sings
> A song that's so old   –*Prince, '7'*

When I come upon a new story or song, it integrates with the symbol-world in my head – and the more permeable a text is, the more imaginative surface area it has, the more points of contact it finds with my private image-world, the deeper it sinks into me, or I into it. Here's *Riddley Walker* by Russell Hoban (RIP):

> Every morning they were counting every thing to see if any thing ben took off in the nite. How many goats how many cows how many measurs weat and barly. Cudnt stop ther counting which wer clevverness and making mor the same. They said, 'Them as counts counts moren them as dont count.'
>
> Counting counting they wer all the time. They had iron then and big fire they had towns of parpety. They had machines et numbers up. They fed them numbers and they fractiont out the Power of things. They had the Nos. of the rain bow and the Power of the air all workit out with counting which is how

they got boats in the air and picters on the wind. Counting clevverness is what it wer.

When they had all them things and marvelsome they cudnt sleap realy they dint have no res. They wer stressing ther self and straining all the time with counting. They said, 'What good is nite its only dark time it aint no good for nothing only them as want to sly and sneak and take our parpety a way.' They los out of memberment who nite wer. They jus wantit day time all the time and they wer going to do it with the Master Chaynjis.

They had the Nos. of the sun and moon all fractiont out and fed to the machines. They said, 'Wewl put all the Nos. in to 1 Big 1 and that wil be the No. of the Master Chaynjis.' They bilt the Power Ring thats where you see the Ring Ditch now. They put in the 1 Big 1 and woosht it roun there come a flash of lite then bigger nor the woal worl and it ternt the nite to day. Then every thing gone black. Nothing only nite for years on end. Playgs kilt peopl off and naminals nor there wernt nothing growit in the groun. Man and woman starveling in the blackness looking for the dog to eat it and the dog out looking to eat them the same. Finely there come day agen then nite and day regler but never like it ben befor. Day beartht crookit out of crookit nite and sickness in them boath.

Now man and woman go afeart by nite afeart by day. The dog all lorn and wishful it keaps howling for the nites whatre gone for ever. It wont show its eyes no mor it wont show the man and woman no 1st knowing. Come Ful of the Moon the sadness gets too much the dog goes mad. It follers on the man and womans track and arga warga if it catches them.

Riddley is a short book but it contains a whole world, or maybe several – the primordial world of men and beasts ('man and woman starveling in the blackness looking for the dog to eat it and the dog out looking to eat them the same…arga warga…')

studded with artifacts, physical and linguistic, of our own world ('the Nos. of the sun and moon all fractiont out and fed to the machines...the Power Ring...'). *Riddley* is set in our postapocalyptic future, and its setting – a second Iron Age dotted with ruins of a grander modern age, which ended in catastrophe – extends the logic of Tolkien's Middle-Earth, where the mythic past irrupts into the falling/fallen present. Indeed, Hoban has a little guy (13-year-old Riddley) walking around the slowly industrializing wild country of a mythic (future) England, 'Inland,' destined to become again something like our world, just as Middle-Earth is Tolkien's legendary primal England, a wild place destined to modernize and thereby ruin itself.

I say all this to give you a sense of the way stories can coexist, *alternating* in and out of your inner sight, and slowly achieve an intense imaginative *simultaneity* that can be harrowing (when my Beacon Hill backalleys became for me Spring-Heeled Jack's London, my solitary late-night walks stopped) but also blissful, transporting. This is Weird epistemology if you like: committing, or just surrendering, to a 'wrong' knowing (but benign), in order to imbue your physical world with new cognitive complexity. ('Apocalyptic time. Mirror time.')

And now I invite you again to hear this music in such terms, to see it *bisociatively,* as a single situation or idea that is perceived in two self-consistent but fundamentally incompatible frames of reference.'[51] Fall 97 is a specific moment in the history of a single band, but also part of the slow tidal movement of a culture – several cultures in fact – and also an element in your

---

[51] Arthur Koestler, *The Act of Creation,* though if you wanna read more of the sort of stuff I'm babbling about, you'll do well to seek out Kenneth Hite's writing on bisociation, for instance in the 'Two-World Minimum' essay in his first *Suppressed Transmission* anthology. If you've never heard of the *Transmission,* do yourself a favour and grab the two collections from Steve Jackson Games. There's a wonderful surprise waiting for you.

own mental listening-library, establishing norms but still able to surprise them, to *contradict itself*...we should cultivate the habit of containing multitudes, just like the man said. And we can, and therefore should, take pleasure in it.

> There is a view by which it can be shown, or more or less demonstrated, that there never has been a coincidence...By a coincidence is meant a false appearance, or suggestion, of relations among circumstances. But anybody who accepts that there is an underlying oneness of all things, accepts that there are no utter absences of relations among circumstances—
>
> Or that there are no coincidences, in the sense that there are no real discords in either colors or musical notes—
>
> That any two colors, or sounds, can be harmonized, by intermediately relating them to other colors, or sounds. (Charles Fort, Wild *Talents*)

The time can become (much more than merely) the music. Dwelling in tension can be the goal; release can be prelude to deeper tension. The show can be a single song in the tale of the tour. Monk says It's always night (or we wouldn't need light) and there can be hidden colours or summer onstage in winter. A river runs beneath the street. The country is a map of what you heard as you drove through nights to each temple in turn; even land fills in line by line in crossing; even open A-major chord a complex snarl of sound, ritual noise, old things conjured. A billion years ago these same sounds rang free somewhere.

Across deep canyons seawaterfilled, or drowned mountains leagues high but hidden, a rumble comes. Dangerous. Too cold to breathe. Dragons swim bloodless and pour forth dark white light from sightless eyes. Slowly a feeling creeps closer. Shapeless and its breath sickly cold. Older than earth out of the deep places of the world. Out of time.

Why not?

it could be the dragons (Blake's beasts) or the light (look upon my works) or the mountains (madness; mist) or the creeping feeling (six the senses beyond our sixth) or the deep places (fly fools) or time (10:00 give or take on a Sunday night as November fell away to the turn of the year and though hidden within a second skeleton of glass and steel among friendly strangers I could still *feel the goddamn cold*...)

the music, i mean,

might be all these things

at once

❤ ☞ ✤ ☞ ✳

Three nights one song, then.

If you can hear into that then I'll just rest here awhile.

It's nearly December, y'know. ('In reality' it's the twelfth of October, chilly outside, steelygrey clouds moving with purpose, though the sun's doing her level best with a bad hand.)

I've always thought the story took a turn after the Worcester shows. Even granting the factual incorrectness of this claim – *which after all flatly contradicts most of what I've already written* – well, that's the colour they take in my mind, so I can't write my way into the December shows without at least acknowledging my own strange overdetermined relationship to them. The way they sweep through (my) private time. (I was at the final Worcester 97 gig, my only Fall Tour show, a great blessing; listening to it now, that post-Free wash of cosmic radiation, I can feel starlight reaching through the noise of day, a hidden pattern; whole worlds coming free...)

Oh by the way:

These three shows are as good as the rest. The music is phenomenal – even falling it rises into something wonderful. I hope you give it a listen[52] and a look.

---

[52] The hourlong Jim jam is available from *livephish.com* on the free promotional release 'Live Bait 3' in glorious soundboard form. You've been warned.

old break

From a long essay I wrote in early 2009:

Phish are the inheritors of an American improvisatory-rock tradition that passes through the Dead and the Allmans, blending their country-rock, R&B, and acid-bluegrass/folk influences with the ambient/textural preoccupations of Pink Floyd and the electric roar and hop of Led Zeppelin. (Barring the hard-rock influence, the Dead unite all of the above influences, and the Dead are obviously a major influence on Phish, arguably though not certainly the single largest musical influence.) In Phish this tradition meets the prog-theatre melodrama of early Genesis, the minimalist world-beat art-rock of Talking Heads, and – crucially – the particular improvisatory and textural modes that thread from Miles's electric bands through every piece of listenable electronica of the last thirty years. While brother bands like Medeski Martin & Wood spent the 90's developing an NYC instrumental hip-hop sound in a jazz context, Phish spent the second half of the decade exploring ambient and dance-beat soundscapes in the tonal language of 70's rock and 80's post-punk. You don't get Phish without Miles or Page/Plant or Robert Townsend, but you also need Peter Gabriel and Brian Eno in there: as Trey Anastasio has said, they didn't set out to be a 'jam band,' they just improvised as a way of extending the complex *compositions* they were playing. The jamming was always an extension of the songwriting, in other words. Which is why the four members of Phish spent fifteen years *constantly* practicing: to learn how to honour the song forms and textures on which their jams would need to build.

The band's later, more loose-limbed rock improvisations bear much more resemblance to what now passes for 'jam band' music than did their pre-watershed (say, pre–1998) improv. And Anastasio's songwriting has gotten more linear, more grounded in a traditional guy-with-guitar form of rock songcraft. But for a while the band was truly unclassifiable – ostentatiously talented prog-jazz barroom rockers playing intricate ten-minute collective improvisations full of hairpin unison rhythmic turns and gnarly dissonances. The band's music has always been a little too cerebral to achieve Miles's challenge of forming the best rock band anyone ever heard, but of all contemporary American rock bands, Phish might come closest. Their improvisations create *entirely new* rock sounds, drawing on everything from Afrobeat funk to deep-country twang to 80's glam. If that seems like a small thing, consider how few bands ever pioneer a *sound*; now consider only those bands that innovate both sonically *and* formally; now ask whether any of those bands of, say, the last half-century play(ed) open-hearted accessible pop music beloved of millions. The Beatles come to mind of course, along with The Police, Pink Floyd, Talking Heads, maybe (*maybe*) The Pixies or somesuch, arguably Sinatra, and several jazz artists (Miles, Coltrane, Bird/Diz). At which point you run out of options fast.

It feels strange to mention Phish in that company. But the evidence, however unconvincing, is there: thousands of hours of high-quality live recordings, more than a dozen albums, a cultural legacy already more than a quarter-century old. You might not like the stuff but it matters, and I'd like to lead you to liking it. I'd like to think we can dig the reasons *why*, too. While we're here.

One of the remarkable things about jazz is that for much of its history its most skilled practitioners and influential figures have also been its most *popular*: Duke Ellington, Miles Davis, John Coltrane, Charles Mingus, Dizzie Gillespie, Charlie Parker, Louis Armstrong, Bill Evans, Count Basie, Ella Fitzgerald, Billie Holiday, Wynton Marsalis (say what you want about 'neoconservatism' but the man is the most ambitious composer and the greatest trumpeter in modern jazz). Indeed, the bestselling album in jazz history is arguably the single greatest jazz LP ever recorded (*Kind of Blue* by the Miles Davis Sextet). Lucky for new listeners! This was true in rock during the Sixties, when the Beatles were both the best and the most popular band on earth, and arguably true during the reign of Michael Jackson (who for a while was making perfect music); and by the way it was true in basketball during Michael Jordan's reign. But things have changed in both jazz and rock/pop, and today's bestselling American music is technically assured but uninteresting. This is a bad state for an art to be in: popularity grants great artists both crucial accountability and a certain impulse to experiment (as Just Entertaining can get awfully boring).

It's a bit hard to know how to categorize Phish; they came up with the insipid alt-rock wave of the 90's, but always had a much more experimental outlook than their (e.g.) college-pop/rock peers in Blues Traveler, Dave Matthews Band, Rusted Root, Spin Doctors, etc. Yet they're not a jazz band – though they did tour for a time, improbably, as the Jonny B. Fishman Jazz Ensemble. By pop/rock standards they're too technical, too quirky; by jazz standards, or that of the more loosely-defined 'improvisatory music' tradition, Phish's stuff is too straightforward – rarely will the band play more than five minutes of 'inaccessible' music. They're too far off the beaten path to achieve jazz popularity and too damn popular to attain rock respectability. And yet there it is, a mountainous body of work as ambitious and multifaceted as any in contemporary music. Their schizoid in-concert medleys anticipated 'mashups,' while their drum-circle improvised builds and by-the-campfire sound are precursors of 'freak folk.' Best of all, Phish's 1986 recordings sound nothing like their 1993 material, which is a world away from their 1998 work, which has little in common stylistically with the band's 2004 stuff; what Miles Davis's epochal, furious, vivisectionist 1965 *Plugged Nickel* sets were to his stately mid–50's source material, Phish's contemporary performances are to their five- or even ten-year-old songlists and styles.

And they've been reinventing themselves in this way for a quarter-century now.

And so there's the band's importance, its biographical scope. The newsreel highlights – 80,000 festival attendees, seven-hour onstage excursions, four-night concert runs without a single repeated song, the monster ticket sales, the two-hundred-date touring years, the marathon psychedelics-heavy practice sessions, the thousands of followers crossing the country each summer and fall carefully taking down setlists and arguing over what constitutes an improvised segue, the most heavily-trafficked Usenet newsgroup (rec.music.phish), the flying hot dog, the *White Album* cover, the 'secret language,' the canonical minitour booked 'because we [the band] were bored' – these trappings are like the giant penny or the robotic dinosaur in the Batcave, part of the story but incidental to the legacy. The legacy is: an American songbook, a mode of improvisation, and an open cooperative interactive fan/band cultural model that's the keystone of a great and *growing* pop-musical counterforce in contemporary America.

So. Why should you care? Why should you listen? How should you listen? Why do I insist?

What does it mean?

Or rather, *What can it mean?*

♥ ☞ ♣ ☞ ✳

When we move from talking about 'altered consciousness,' with its implicit therapeutic goal of returning to 'normal,' or even 'expanded consciousness' with its naive emphasis on thinking one's way to *correctness* (it's a political/religious term, alas), and come around to acknowledging the possibility of *alternate* consciousnesses – different frameworks for understanding the world and (literally) different mechanisms for processing relationships between things – we break away from the zero-sum parochialism and protectionism of religious/spiritual dogma. 'Learning' might be defined, if perhaps a little glibly, as 'non-zero-sum thinking.' Walter Murch tells the startling story of his two weeks listening to nothing but Gregorian Chant at work, at the end of which he was driven out of his skull by a blast of incoherent, unparseable noise – which turned out to be Bach's *Passion of St Matthew*. One is tempted to think Murch *constrained* his consciousness through this experiment, but it's more evenhanded to say he simply reprogrammed his listening apparatus as a survival mechanism, acclimated himself to the environment in which he was working – *adapted* to the flow of aural information around him. He relearned soon enough how to comprehend Baroque music and modern music alike, and – here's the crucial point – the experience of radical circumscription altered his sense of the place and possibility of sound. (Murch is one of the great Hollywood film editors, and is responsible for, among other things, the astonishing avant-garde soundscapes in George Lucas's *THX–1138*.)

The point of which is just this: just as immersion in water causes certain survival mechanisms to kick in, and immersion in a foreign-speaking culture revitalizes our language-acquisition apparatus (witness the profanity on *Deadwood*, or spend two months in Spain), *musical* immersion makes available to us certain forms of consciousness – and long-form improvisatory music is an ideal tool for producing these alternate states. Its openendedness lifts certain expectations of closure and precision/unity (just as Modernist literary abstraction/formalism prepared readers for the deferral or denial of satisfaction). Its seemingly arbitrary complication can open us up to a kind of simultaneous experience of melody and harmony, as for instance when John Coltrane would play a simple five note melody with each pair of notes separated by a complex cascading arpeggio, which functioned as colour and texture rather than traditional melodic content – see his inspired *Interstellar Space* for the purest examples of this kind of musical storytelling. The different tempos and rhythms of in-the-moment personal expression in jazz and other improvised musics free the audience from the bang-bang-bang rhythm of traditional music, allowing listeners to comprehend the music at their own speed according to their own free-floating focus – which is in turn *more likely* to correspond directly to the human-scale shifts in attention and intention of improvised performance than to the preordained formal shifts of throughcomposed music. Improvisatory forms allow the musicians to testify to their experiences *as musicians* more directly than do written forms, which first and foremost testify to their writers' experiences *as writers* – all live musical performance liberates the music to a degree, but jazz and its sister forms privilege something like *faith-based* expression, in (this always needs saying) forms and fashions reflective of a particular black American experience.

Yet the best improvisation *does* partake of the clean collective tension-and-release of written music. The root of Western harmony is the resolving cadence, V-I. (Think of the first two notes of the *Star Wars* theme, or the opening of 'Eine Kleine Nachtmusik,' or 'Here Comes the Bride.') Eight out of ten doo-wop songs progress along traditional lines: I-vi-IV-V-I; 'I've Got Rhythm' is practically a long cycle of V-I cadences, shifted up or down the scale. Its musical particulars aren't important – what's important is that Western music goes like this: UP. THEN DOWN. Or down, then up – or out then in or viceversa, louder then softer, more then less, nasty then neat, fast-slow-fast or slow-fast-slow. The best moment on *Remain in Light* is the refrain of 'Once in a Lifetime' – 'Letting the days go by /Let the water hold me down' – but half the reason it hits you so hard on the album is that the first three songs get faster and *faster* and **FASTER** and then…'Once in a Lifetime' just lets the bottom out and dives into a midtempo groove suitable for, among other things, relaxing after fifteen minutes of increasingly frenzied dancefloor action. (It's a party album.)

First rule of good sex is 'What's your hurry?' Second rule is 'Well OK, but you still gotta *get* there.' Which combine to 'Tension and release want each other,' and it's the same with music. Nature abhors a vacuum, our expectations create musical vacuums, and in writing or performance musicians learn to fill those vacuums, then learn to play *toward* them, to make their instantaneous responses seem continuous, to craft musical logics into which various forms of expression can be fit without seeming stilted or unnatural.

Listening to improvised music means listening for those logics: the way a melody will outline a chord change with only a slight movement instead of jumping arbitrarily from one root to another, or how a drummer will echo the bassist's line in his kick drum, carrying the rhythm forward while the bassist outlines a complementary line (thereby *doubling* the bass momentarily, multiplying its presence, the bassist duetting with himself). Or getting past the weirdness of Miles Davis's sparse trumpet bleats to hear how he goads the other musicians, or alerts them to an interesting confluence of keyboard and bass, or accents a particularly rich rhythm with the tonal equivalent of 'Come on now, more, motherfucker!' Or how a section of Phish's improv might sound thin, the notes crammed into a narrow register, because the pianist is laying out and the bassist is sticking to the highest range of his instrument during this passage so that when he splashes down to his low E string with a thunderous BOMBLE AND GLORP it has all the impact of a jet plane arriving. Getting with improvised music means the cats up onstage are just playing G-Em-Am-D over and over like the goddamn Ramones but then all of a sudden something just *ticks* over and it all seems a little more intense, and you were paying close attention and noticed just in time that the drummer had signaled with a roll down the tom-toms, so that when the guitarist switched from barre chords way up on the guitar's neck – clipped and precise, accompanists' chords – to ringing open-string chords at the bottom like every guitarist learns on Day One when it looks like everything could be possible and for once you're right, it is; and that's opened up the sound of the song, the different guitar voicing means the same chords sound twice as full, it sounds like a choir has opened up on these chords. And now the keyboard is signaling the coming end of the tune with a *suspension*, a held note atop a series of chords, *suitable for singing along at the top of your lungs, baby,* like a written permission slip from Mom and Dad saying 'Go nuts, dear.'

Which you do, and now you have a new idea as to *why*. Not a particularly complicated one – this isn't music theory in the institutional sense so much as a vernacular theory of listenership – but hopefully it's a *rich* language, one that opens itself up growing, which opens *you* up as well. Hopefully.

One of the wonderful things about musical improvisation is that it partakes of our narrativizing faculties (near as we can tell, humans are the only species crazy and needy enough to make Time into Story), but also liberates us of the arbitrary time constraints – the very specific, sometimes even perverse relationship to time – characterizing composed music. Yet great improv has *shape*, it's got a *groove* (even if that groove isn't readily identifiable as rhythm), it gives you something to latch onto. Seeming purposelessness allows for the expression of hidden, individual, shared purpose. Improvisation is a set of practices allowing performers unusually direct means to experience and express faith. Improvisatory listening affords the audience a variant of those experiences, and an unusually high degree of participation in those expressions.

That's part of why jazz is so sexy: because the logic of assembly seems to reside in and rest with the listener to a large degree, the physical and cognitive experience of listenership is heightened; and because the performance proceeds within the logic and limits of group physical expression, the audience responds not to the written shape of music on the page (interpreted in the moment) but to the sweep, sway, parry, and caress of noise-making itself. You come out of a jazz show feeling like you've been through something along *with* the musicians. Same goes for rock and pop and classical music too – but the improvisor's complex relationship to her bandmates is bound to the time of performance itself. Ten minutes into a performance, free or not, you're a long damn way from where you set out, and if you've lost sight of the chords and the rhythm pattern and (oh yeah) the lyrics or what have you, then what's left is: the memory of the thing, and one another. When the keyboardist lays out for a few bars the only difference between her and the audience is who paid to be here. You can listen with the same ears.

Listening eyes tightly closed in the whirl of the middle of the moment of it is sexy; swaying to an after-midnight beat you make together is sexy. Hearing the hidden language of it – speaking to the music with the ring and human of the body, grasping the secret logic and array of expression – is very, very sexy.

On which subject I definitely can't do better than this:

> Strip to your underwear if you're not in black tie. Get obscene if you want, but never casual. You feel an urge? Touch its pain, wrap yourself around it. Don't put on airs. What you seem must be what you are, and what you are is a mess, honey, but that's okay, as long as you wear it inside. Look sharp! Don't slouch. See anyone slouching here? Stay poised, taut, on guard. Listen to your nerves. It's zero hour. Anxiety encroaches, wave after wave, with every squeeze of the bandoneon. Already twisted by the contraposto of uprightness and savagery, this new tango turns the screw even tighter with its jazz dissonances and truncated phrasings. No relief. No quarter. At zero hour only passion can save you. Time is flowing backward and forward into the vortex. From the rooms come a warm air and a choked melody of syncopated

> gasps. Something throbs. A vein under your skin. It's inside you now, this bordello virus, this pleasure that tastes so much of anger and grief. When you find pools of pure, sweet light, bathe in their waters, balm for your lacerations. For the whiplash scars the bandoneon is leaving on your soul. If this were the old milonga of the slums, or those popular songs about painted faces and purloined love, you could let distance sketch a smile on your lips. Cheap irony. You won't get away that easy. This music is for you. It always had you in mind, your habits, your twitches, the tiny blood vessels bursting inside you when you hide what you feel. So walk in the parlor, bring your friend or come alone. Come hear the master as he unravels the wind inside the box, as he presses the growling tiger that threatens to embrace him and shapes the beast into a purring kitten. And tiger again. And kitten. It's all a game. You're going to play it too, you're going to dance with the tiger. Don't worry, your life is in danger. Remember your instructions. Listen up. And suffer, motherfucker, this is the tango.

That's Enrique Fernandez, the liner notes to Piazzolla's *Tango: Zero Hour*. That is the language we'd like to speak: 'Get obscene if you want, but never casual.' 'Don't worry, your life is in danger.' Don't be afraid of crossing unseen borders; it's happened already if you've left your house at all. Everyone shares the risk. What's risked is only *yesterday*, where we've come from, what we think and thought we were doing for. The reward is variegation and complication of what comes next. Receiving the next expression or eventuality in its full complexity is the desired experience, the thing itself. Not a musical 'goal,' some imputed motivation or end-state, but a way of doing. We don't want to 'be happy' but to *do joyfully*.

It's goddamn dance music we're talking about. So dance.

Music is made of notes and silence, sure, but the meaning of music is made of musical relationships – between moments, or a pair of notes, or two chordal colours – which are perceived differently by any two listeners. So then there's *that*: the relationship between two listeners, recipients, who must then negotiate the meaning of the music between them. Who struggle to make their experiences communicable, to find common experiential language which might substitute for various musical languages. We search for emotional shorthand to replace craftsmen's productive/technical jargon, which itself is a shorthand standing in for deeper communication *in process*. The relationships between musical elements are what we hear without hearing; what we listen to and what we listen *for* are related in practice but not identity, like the football and the 40-yard line. Two different sorts of thing bound by purpose.

The dialectic of tension and release is the motive force of improvised music. No still lives.

I have a friend who's been to maybe three times as many Phish shows as I have. We can mention specific versions of particular songs – 'the Providence Bowie,' or 'that second set at the Palace in 1997' – and catch immediate transport to another state of mind. Yet to listen again to those pieces of music is to refresh our understanding of them. They aren't solved problems. First time you look at a webpage you grab it live from the server. Next time you might simply reload the version you downloaded – a cached copy. The rehearsal of habit. You explicitly tell the machine to make it new and it'll do so cheerily. The cache is a survival mechanism and we *need* to overgo it to keep living. Living *is* growth. Stop growing and that's – the other thing, I suppose. Improv allows creators to testify in a direct way to the processes of growth, variation, evolution, which make up life. 'Nature knows neither creation nor destruction – only transformation.' Which is why it's OK to play chord changes, even to play them your whole life long. And OK to play riffs at a free jazz show. But better altogether, I'd say, to embrace change itself. Iteration.

In my iTunes library I've got 24 versions of 'You Enjoy Myself,'[53] the archetypal Phish song, and I imagine I've got another 20 or so on tape. (My collection puts me somewhere in the fat part of the Gaussian in terms of live Phish collections, sizewise – the largest are of course near-complete, 1,000-hour collections are surprisingly numerous, and 100+ hours of tapes was a common milestone in the late 90's, even before instant lossless digital copies. And never mind the Deadheads.) Why in the world would someone want forty-odd recordings of a single song – particularly a song that routinely runs twenty-five minutes in concert and *almost never* varies in terms of overall structure? 'Fetishism' is the too-easy answer, and we can do better.

I'd say first that I collect live Phish recordings because they offer a particular ratio of risk and danger to comfort and familiarity: I can sing nearly all of Phish's 300+ originals and most of their covers, and when a given jam takes off I have a feel for the sound, can often predict the first few licks – am rewarded with a moment of *thinking like the band*. But after a moment, the chaotic variation of live performance has begun, and the four musicians are recombining ever-shifting atomic elements along familiar lines but according to unique timebound impulses. And it's the moments of *departure* that appeal most strongly – my predictive powers in a way that reaffirms my faith, like the sun not

---

[53]Lots more now!

failing to rise but rising *red*, or the rain coming in unexpected torrents but still not raining *frogs* or anything. This isn't just the illusion of difference. I still make distinctions between versions, can still instantly identify jams by period or even specific date. Nor are they distinctions without a difference – you might not hear the variety but it's there, as the musicians would happily tell you. Yet the small differences add up and multiply, pile atop one another, and the evolution of a tune over the course of a single tour becomes a new source of pleasure. Fandom offers new avenues to pleasure, and interesting (non-juvenile) fandom lets us see *both* the world of differences between e.g. two versions of 'YEM,' on the one hand, and the continuity into which they both fit, on the other. Tension and release: the continuity makes the variety meaningful, the variety makes the continuity worthwhile. The meaning of the music is path-dependent: 'Tube' and 'Wolfman's Brother' and 'Tweezer' might over three nights all end up in similar-sounding polyrhythmic funk jams, but the process by which each song transforms is the real object of interest. The contortions that understanding requires. And, since you're probably not all alone in your listening, the second sort of contortion, for mutual benefit, required to *share* meaning.

For me to put this down I have to bend – and bend words – into shapes I hadn't expected to require or imagine. Becoming new things is exciting, and exploring the fullness of a heretofore-unimagined new state of being and action is *doubly* exciting. You can create that newness in your own mind by paying attention to each moment of what's ongoing, by attending to the continuity of events so that any sharp change or sudden break in pattern stands out. Humans have built-in edge-finding capabilities: we're good at seeing the difference between black and white regions of a visual field, for instance, to distinguish between objects and backgrounds. But as we expand our vocabularies and deepen our understanding of individual things – *acquiring expertise*, in other words – we can see new edges, hook in to smaller differences, stop short just as surely at a previously-invisible break or fillip. Like sharpening a knife – a well-honed blade can slip easily through tiny breaks in surfaces that had theretofore presented themselves as continuous. We can see – and slide into – the invisible grain of things.

The difference between the kind of listening I'm gabbing about and the hip-hop producer/indie rock fan's obsession with guitar sound and synth textures is the difference between Joyce writing down lists of puns because puns are neat and lists are neat, and Joyce writing *Finnegans Wake* in a *language* of puns because he wanted to give people the feeling of a waking dream. Tiny variations in time and human expression are not the same as tiny variations in effect, in *mechanism*. The difference between the improvisor's craft and the producer's is like the perilous gulf between the playwright's work and the actor's. No meaning without the writer; no show without the actor. Maybe *fewer* meanings, but still. Which could you do without?

Not that you shouldn't also worry about that stuff. (I'm a chauvinist in this matter without question but I'm not a complete idiot.) But I'm asking you to open up to another sort of creation – pardon me, transformation – that takes place not just in the moment of acquisition but *every* moment. Music you could turn around and start making yourself. People noises. The return of Everybody Singing.

Do you walk around with iPod earphones in, drowning out the world? Do you make music sitting in front of your laptop screen? What you do is not the same thing you do at the Vanguard with Trane on stage gutting out a solo – or for that matter what Trane does. The danger is different.

Maybe someone else can write an essay hectoring you about that stuff. I'm not grown up enough; I grow and go another way.

Why is sharing all this stuff important or even worthwhile at all? 'Starting with the band and radiating outward the message here seems to be, "We are not alone."' I want the message to pass through you. I want the message to pass through me. 'We tell each other stories in order to live.' Music is a story.

❤ ☞ ❈ ☞ ✳

The core principle of Zen – total awareness and acceptance of which would seem to constitute Enlightenment, as I understand it – is twofold: all things exist independently, and all things are interconnected. Independence and interdependence are total, inescapable, and simultaneous, and aren't contradictory as we might falsely believe. Another way of putting it: 'The universe doesn't revolve around you. *Nothing* revolves around you.' What a wonderfully irresponsible way of being and seeing. Get up on the bandstand now. The Zen direction is 'Listen totally, speak honestly.' And out of listening and speaking, notice which comes first. It's 'common sense,' which is often just a defensive term for 'do as I say not as I do.' Aspirational wisdom in folk terms. Those Zen guys are all crazy and many of them possess the power to levitate, which doesn't make them wrong, just creepy.

Zen awareness doesn't seem to produce complex art; that requires ego and the lust for conquest/understanding, it seems. Great art comes from the tension: complex means for attaining simplicity. Is that a definition of 'elegance'? Well how would I know, I write long essays about rock'n'roll music.

When the members of Phish split up for the first time in 2000, one of the forces pushing them apart was the fact that they employed many of their friends in the ever-growing Phish organization – meaning that they couldn't stop even for a time without hurting their friends careerwise, moneywise, emotionally. They were the party and no one wants to stop the party. The 2000–2002 break was helpful and necessary but didn't solve all their problems; in 2004 the band split up, *thinking* this time that it might be permanent, because of a combination of drug problems and the same old it's-all-too-damn-big feeling. (One suspects, when listening to the awkward and unsatisfying August 2004 shows, that drug addiction was the main problem.) The 2004–2009 break has dissipated the entire Phish organization; the band has a new manager now, new goals, a new approach to touring, and many fewer attachments to the 'scene.'

But drugs and family and business concerns aside, another thing is readily apparent from even a quick listen to Phish's voluminous live and studio output: that kind of music is *tiring*. In its early years the band was (in)famous for doing schematic rehearsal exercises onstage, for instance at frat party shows – a bit like a championship pro team playing a local club and passing time by playing keepaway with *themselves* rather than deigning to engage the locals. Which is to say: they were very very good, and they needed a bigger challenge, and they could be a little bit *jerky*, but the jerkiness came out of devotion to something they couldn't (yet) express – something like monks needing human contact but coming to prefer the contact *only* of other monks, no longer even missing the outside world. They were playing a different game. The game for Phish was: listen to one another so totally that personal expression is totally subsumed in the collective statement. In interviews the members of Phish have said that talking to people other than their bandmates seems curiously slow, because they're used to having simultaneous four-way conversations; *taking turns* is almost a foreign concept, and a musically inadequate one. (Guest musicians with Phish rarely rise to the level of the band, though musicians who share this virtuosic/ascetic aesthetic, like Béla Fleck, do beautifully.) To do this physically demanding thing for three hours a night while also playing recognizable songs, *entertaining* several thousand fans sure to pick apart your every musical choice on the way to the next tour stop…it's draining, it has to be.

Which is why two weeks at the Zendo isn't going to get you anywhere, by the way, and Hollywood Kabbalists really are laughable (even more than *other* Kabbalists!). If you're in, you're in for the long haul, and it's brutal *by necessity*. There's no easy Zen. 'Suffer, motherfucker, this is the tango.' There's no such thing as easy discipline. No such thing as 'nurturing your creative spirit' either, only hard work. Muses are fictional creatures. Creativity is response to constraint; it comes after work. From it. There are ways to have fun and look like you're making art, but the craft is something else.

Interconnection is hard work, and recognizing the independence of others is hard work. I suppose I'm trying to convince you that Phish's musical ethic is one that recognizes and pursues these difficult realizations in a particularly conscious, *direct* way – that delving into deep open-eared musical improvisation as player *or* listener connotes a particular way of seeing the world, apprehending the rippling lattice of things, the great *canopy* that sweeps overhead. Which isn't meant as spiritual gobbledygook of the 'cosmic message' sort; the band isn't 'in touch' with anything other than one another. That's enough. We have no idea just how much that is. It's enough.

All these special claims I'm making about improvisatory music might well be made, in altered forms, for other musical languages and forms. *I don't know.* (You've probably figured that out already.) What you can find here, I hope, is a pointer, a map. When the lights go down and the music rises up, all those present are afforded the chance to be part of a collective expression of faith in one another. It belongs in the same continuum as leaving your car door unlocked while you're at the grocery store, or trusting a lover to have your best interests at heart: maybe it's stupid, sure, but *what if it works?* The questions we can't answer are the ones that'll be left to us when business and time have claimed everything else. It's so, so exciting not to know the answer to this one: *What if it works?*

Count off with me, then: 1, 2, 3, 4 –

and then sum

Fall 97 was Phish's Europe 72 – that once-in-a-lifetime moment when the band reaches simultaneous peak technical proficiency, peak fluidity, and peak intensity, while hitting upon *new exploratory methods*. The Dead had Dark Star and The Other One (along with Truckin')[54] as 'open jamming' vehicles in those days; Phish had Tweezer, Bag, Ghost, Gin, 2001, Stash, Jim…all of a sudden they were interested in letting *all* their songs overflow their forms. And unlike in 1998–2004, in Fall 97 Phish hadn't yet started to perform sloppy renditions of their written tunes. 'Correctness' was still taken for granted.

That was the supernova. The instauration. For a moment there was only future again. Fall 1997 changed the meaning and value of the music that they'd played before, and inescapably set the terms for the music they'd play after.

They had to break up for five years to play another way – that was the extraordinary, unexpected weight of the new thing. Discovery.

This book isn't *strictly* or solely about that tour or the music it produced; Phish's 1997 Fall Tour is the center of gravity around which this story revolves. But I can't imagine writing such a

---

[54]Playin' in the Band doesn't really count: open-ended in length, yeah, but how often did a Playin' jam turn away from its original structure in April/May 72? The only *long* jams played on that tour were DStar/TOOne/Truckin' and the Pigpen raveups, which weren't exactly 'open' jams either.

book about any other tour in the band's history. Maybe you could – and I wish you would. But I can't.

In all its imperfection, this music is perfect to me.

and furthermore

DECEMBER 2 AND 3, PHILLY

I: Buried Alive > Disease > Makisupa, Chalkdust, Ghost > Divided, Dirt > Taste, Star Spangled Banner **II:** Mike's > Simple > Dog Faced Boy > Ya Mar > Weekapaug, Bouncin', Char0 **E:** Ginseng, Sample

I: PYITE > My Soul, Drowned, Old Home Place, Gumbo > 2001 > YEM, **II:** Bowie > Possum > Jam > Caspian > Frankenstein > Hood **E:** Crossroads

Nine more shows, including these two top-shelf doozlaes, in just twelve days. Everyone was different then. (For one thing, no one yet used the word 'doozlae.')

A fella named Felix Baumgartner jumped from a capsule at the edge of space yesterday. He wore a spacesuit, for obvious reasons – there's almost no air **24 miles** above the ground.

> After flying to an altitude of 39,045 meters (128,100 feet) in a helium-filled balloon, Felix Baumgartner completed Sunday morning a record breaking jump for the ages from the edge of space, exactly 65 years after Chuck Yeager first broke the sound barrier flying in an experimental rocket-powered airplane. The 43-year-old Austrian skydiving expert also broke two other world records (highest freefall, highest manned balloon flight), leaving the one for the longest freefall to project mentor Col. Joe Kittinger.

> Baumgartner landed safely with his parachute in the desert of New Mexico after jumping out of his space capsule at 39,045 meters and plunging back towards earth, hitting a maximum of speed of 1,342.8 km/h through the near vacuum of the stratosphere before being slowed by the atmosphere later during his 4:20 minute long freefall. Countless millions of people around the world watched his ascent and jump live on television broadcasts and live stream on the Internet.[55]

Why jump out of a damned spaceship? Seriously! Five years of preparation for four minutes of falling, during which you're in serious danger of falling unconscious and dying? Surely no one takes seriously the idea that the point is to have better stories to tell – you can always *make them up* – and it's not like these physical risk-takers (dude's a skydiver by vocation, near as I can tell) are leading double lives as philosopher-poets, spreading wisdom to the world.

So what's the point? Mustn't there be one?

From here we go mundane: what's the point of a tune like 2001? Where's it *going*? It's a dance break – one chord for ten or fifteen minutes. It's a 'jam' only in the sense that it's only got a short written part, but there aren't any really *out-there* versions of the song. You'd look to other tunes (Tweezer, Twist, Stash?) for mind expansion; 1997-era performances of 2001 were prickly and detailed enough to hold attention but weren't really dynamic enough to do anything with it. They *dwell* in fast motion: the beat starts up, you dance, the final refrain finishes, you stop dancing.

If what you dig about coffee isn't caffeine, but *coffee* – you drink for the experience of drinking, for the discernible approach of that psychoactive buzz rather than the increase in utility it

---

[55]http://redbullstratosnewsroom.com

gives you – then the answer is pretty clear: those 10–15 minutes are their own reward. They have a useful side effect (bringing band and audience into a shared mindstate) but their 'goal' is just their being.

When you hear someone complaining about Phish songs going on forever, or all sounding the same, or noodling pointlessly; or when some lazy bourgeois writer carries on about whether things have value in themselves; you point those swine at this here paragraph. Or the ones just above, I guess.

The December 2nd Philly show, particularly its beloved (but not quite famous among fans) second set, expresses something like pure, unself-conscious joy. There's a raucous Mike's jam, through which Fish threads a snakelike syncopated pulse that'll form the backbone of the whole set; the jam grooves and roars and gives way, after twenty finely-detailed minutes, to a lovely Simple. There's a busy but sweet-natured Trey/Page duet; then comes a dazzling Trey-led segue into Dog Faced Boy, and Fishman keeps a sprightly rimshot beat clicking beneath an even more good-natured performance of that light-comic song. After a moment's peaceful outro glide, Trey seems to wanna funk onward, but thankfully he thinks better of it, and his add6 rhythm strut leaps ass-first into the ol' familiar VI-major calypso bounce of Ya Mar.

The Ya Mar jam takes a turn from its usual welcoming smiley-major chord progression to an insinuating minor-blues feel; Fishman works light-fingered magic on the drum riser, somehow integrating both the good-kinda-crazy syncopations outta Mike's Song and the clip-clop canter of Dog Faced Boy into Ya Mar's poolside bounce…and as Trey's solo goes feral and an intensifying full-band jam coalesces around Fish's hip drum hop, a familiar riff pops up to sniff the air, dives back down, then reemerges a moment later as Weekapaug Groove springs joyfully to life.

That tune is nothing special, y'know, just a much-needed breather after the magic, just (oh let's see) fifteen minutes of galactobeat science and hair-raising funk and rock-roar distortion assault, just the nastiest and friendliest *and* most perfectly integrated and flawlessly executed multipart Weekapaug in a year that wasn't exactly what you'd call Weekapaug's *downtime*...

It's one of those second sets where everyone would've understood if the band had taken a year off from music afterward, to just smile and drink tea and do yoga and be loving and proud. And that's without even mentioning the first set, which offers up an absolutely *disgusting* dance jam in Ghost (one of the most successful, which is maybe to say *authenticwhateverthatmeans*, funk grooves of the year) and a very kind Disease > Makisupa up/down pairing to make sure none of the stoners get too *winded* from the brain-shattering dance grooves going...

More than ever I think that the big rock-exorcism sets on November 23rd and 26th represent a real turning point for the band. After Hampton's funk-ambient purification and the Jimi Angry Hendrix séances in Winston-Salem and Hartford, the weekend in Worcester could serve a low-pressure post-holiday hangout scene, a kind of family vacation – and the Philly shows were just as intense as the final Worcester gig, without being imbalanced or abrasive. They overflow with positive energy, going deep (that Gumbo > 2001 is a dark dream, and dig the damn dance jam outta Drowned!) but keeping spirits up.

Even Bowie manages to thrash and meander and finally amble amiably into a cathartic Possum – which isn't enough, Trey wanna get further down, to wrest fire and smoke from his wah pedal, force Page to get into some thoroughly *un-Christian* business with his clavinet right there in front of all those people, those *families* for Christ's sake…

At this point in the tour every preconception has been permanently disposed of. (It's a story, remember? It *means something.*) The flip side is that from here on out there's maybe less to *discover*, I think; when Trey calls for a second Tube jam after the close of Tube proper, it doesn't feel like the natural order of things has changed – it's just 'a funk jam,' which at that point they've already done (I forgive you!) and which also presents something like a revisitation of a *solved problem,* if you like…and the longass first-set Disease on December 11 sounds more tired than exploratory, the next night's Tweezer > Train Song less a wise response to energy than a rapid deflation…

I do love the rest of the month's music, don't get me wrong; the gods keep smiling through 'til New Year's Eve. But even if the 'best set' (to me!) of the tour was yet to come, it's hard (for me!) to shake the feeling that at this point in the band's history, they broke less new ground with each passing year – from now on it's lower information density, thicker sonics, the extension of minimalist principles to every aspect of the music, total characterization of the rhythmic/ambient spaces first given names on *this* tour. I'm almost certain that's just my editorial imposition rather than an 'objective' account; I mean *duh;* but I offer you this proposal, this kinda weird gesture at some notion off in the conceptual distance, as a possibility of hearing this musical story. I don't think it's a *happy* story – quite the opposite, I think that as Phish careened toward, and then staggered past, their millennial apotheosis in the Everglades, they (and their parasitic fans and hangers-on) ate away at what was true and good about the music and culture they made – but then even a story of glorious dissolution can bring joy. Even an unhappy one.

Remember, remember:

> But if you ever stopped a Hancock recording and looked at a few measures of what he's playing, you'd be floored. The voice leadings are filled with all these ideas. It doesn't sound complicated, but it's a more mature, elegant palette of emotions. These guys can hit an emotional chord that a lesser player couldn't…

I readily admit that I'm making up this climax/dissolution narrative for whatever personal reasons, which have nothing to do with the music (except insofar as it's the soundtrack to My Own Story, which even I know I shouldn't waste your time with) (though yes, it's too late; no surprise there).

But I like its shape.

Fuck it though, I'll probably get to the half-hour Simple on December 9th and just be all like SO UNDERRATED THIS IS THE HIGH POINT WHAT BLISS, SOMETHING SOMETHING PRETENSION SOMETHING and you'll be all like DUDE BUT YOU SAID and I'll be like DON'T TALK TO YOUR BOOKS and you'll be like but then I'll be like and the music, blessedly, will be whatever it was and wants and will.

❤ ☞ ♣ ☞ ✳

Something about the Philadelphia Bowie before we go on. This was and is one of the Big News jams of the tour – a 26-minute Bowie that segues organically into Possum, a pairing the band would repeat in much less scintillating fashion during the NYE run just a few weeks later.

Phish have gone deep with Bowie plenty of times over the years – in the mid–90s it was one of their improvisatory heavy hitters, a wide-open modal jam that coasts along on a brisk ride-cymbal beat, with Fishman wielding a lot of power over the feel of the jam just through his snare-hit placement. Mike's bass can keep to an easy sway until he's ready to push the jam forward, and the whole rumbling rolling machine responds smoothly to any player's percussive pressure or hesitation. Indeed, my favourite Bowies tend to start out a little reluctant, a little shapeless – ideally with Fishman providing a rhythmless wash at the beginning, keeping things low and eerie while steam gathers, and only striking out into the jam proper when everyone in the arena's *dying* for it.

What's interesting about *this* jam, though, what sets it apart from, say, the monumental 11/26/94 Bowie, a now-familiar bit of 'psychedelia' featured on the August 2008 'From the Archives' show which circulates in delicious SBD form, is that none of the players lashes out *against* the song's form at any time. 20-odd minutes into that November 94 Bowie there's a vacuum cleaner solo from Fish, beneath which the other three players provide cabaret accompaniment. Over the next few minutes they play a sludgy proto-'space jam' (!),[56] a Simple-esque passage, clav-overdrive a la Weekapaug, and one more interminable distorted hurryup jam – a series of musical notions that feel *to me now* like evasions, rather than elaborations, of the original tune.

Despite being 'unfinished' in formal terms, the Philly 97 Bowie feels more coherent, more *complete* in an aesthetic or emotional sense, than the 11/26/94 performance. What some listeners ('haters'?) hear as monotony, I hear as continuity: the musicians proceed according to an emotional logic within which

---

[56]Don't get excited, it never takes flight – the music maintains a puckish cluttered dissonance, and curls back at its edges as the tempo picks up. A lot of this is on Trey: he just didn't leave *space* back then. It took him a long time start making spacious music. A cold wind blows through the long pauses in tracks like the 11/26/94 Bowie; or laughter echoes (cf. the classic 12/29/94 Bowie, even longer than the two we're discussing but not, I think, a deeper performance). These days, I'll take the coherence and continuity of the later performances over the science-far ostentation of Phish's mid–90s psychedelia…

subtly varying rhythms in a steady tempo have a greater impact than the harsher discontinuities of the earlier version. When the band transitions from tightly wound E-minor into blissful A-D glide (the transition begins around the 17:00 mark), you can feel the whole room exhaling at once: instead of playing games with the crowd's attention and patience, the musicians are flowing smoothly, continuously, between pleasurable tension and pleasurable release.

But crucially, you (I mean 'I') get the sense that it doesn't really matter whether this Bowie ever made it to A-major – think again of the Winston-Salem Stash, which 'resolves' its D-minor deferrals, via a circuitous and rocky harmonic path, in…a remorselessly nervewracking D-minor goblin march, fully five minutes of ominous rumble and Halloween-minor creepout. When *that* jam finally gives way to NICU, it's like draining pus from a sore: the poisonous atmosphere of Stash gives way slowly to NICU's inappropriately cheerful Eb-major skitter only after 40-odd seconds of harrowing bitonality. That period of unstable coexistence is *as much the point* of the musical exercise as any 'bliss' of relief. The Philly Bowie has this same quality of emotional fortitude and mature patience: it lingers in dark, then revels in light, without giving a false feeling of essential difference between the two. It's a grownup game. (It also sounds, in that gorgeous final segment, a lot like the transitional jams from the previous night – which doesn't exactly *endanger* my affection.)

I actively dislike the song Possum – a waste of emotional energy I admit – but the Bowie > Possum segue feels like the most natural thing in the world, like Trey suddenly *remembers* that the songs fit together, rather than trying to shove the square Possum-peg into the round, uhh, Bowie-hole.

I'd like to remove that image from your mind if at all possible.'

> Like everything else in our bodies and minds, Nature built a certain amount of sloppiness and error into pattern matching. Pattern matching malfunctions (or more precisely, over-functions) in a number of related ways. The next step up from simple pattern matching is pareidolia, the mistaken matching of pattern within randomness. This is what makes people see faces on Mars, or the Virgin Mary in a grilled cheese sandwich. A linked category of error is apophenia, the detection of nonexistent connections between phenomena. Apophenia manifests itself in the belief in "lucky socks" and conspiracy theories alike. Time-series apophenia is called "hindsight bias" or "the narrative fallacy." The construction of narrative – this happened, so that happened – is seemingly inherent in human psychology. Where life is, in actuality, "just one damn thing after another," we see a story, a story driven by the narrative thrust of True Love, guardian angels, our Destiny…or malevolent cults of Cthulhu worshipers. (Kenneth Hite, *Dubious Shards*)

> Any fact becomes important when it's connected to another. The connection changes the perspective; it leads you to think that every detail of the world, every voice, every word written or spoken, has more than its literal meaning, that it tells us of a Secret.

> The rule is simple: Suspect, only suspect. (Umberto Eco, *Foucault's Pendulum*)

Chris Kuroda's light show is a big part of the attraction of *seeing* (funny word!) a Phish show, vs 'just getting the tapes.' Some folks think the lights take away from the 'experience of the music'; I think that's a piss-poor account of the show. It's not as if your other senses shut down when you close your eyes to listen – your showgoing experience is still heavily dependent on ambient sounds, smells, memories, anticipation, your senses of balance and proximity...

So there's no 'pure' musical experience to be had, either way, and in any case the lights are *totally rad*. So back to my point:

Good as the lights are, they're only part of the experience – indeed, a small part even of the *visual* component of the show, never mind the multisensory tidal wave that arrives each instant of being, y'know, physically present in 'the world.' You bring so much with you into the space, do so much to shape your experience before the music even begins...and the 'ideal' isn't to suppress this complex cognitive prep-work, it's to shape it, to to shape your habits of body and mind, so you don't screw yourself out of a good time.

Thing is, this work doesn't have to be *neutral:* you can do more than just stay out of your own way. There's a hell of a lot of behavioral psychedelics available to you – patterns and methods which can add dimensions to your experience, from the narrative to the erotic to the inappropriately competitive (some idiots think the *number* of Phish shows you've attended measures something more important than what you hear)...

Believers. Scary yes because they don't quail as you do but the shape their madness takes can frame other fills, structure even the giving of self, giving away yes which is more-making, which is more *life* (and 'more life' is angels' tongue for *blessing*, no wonder we say of children 'what a blessing you are')...[57]

---

[57] The 'Book of J' is the original source text for the Pentateuch (which forms the first five 'books' of the Christian Bible), extended and revised by other writers over several centuries. David Rosenberg and Harold Bloom's book of the same name is a translation, critical commentary, and polemic which I can't summarize. The Blessing, God's divine favour first bestowed upon Abram (Abraham), is in Bloom's account the wonderfully simple phrase 'more life,' in a variety of senses (long earthly life, many children, continued tribal existence, *richness* of being, etc.). Tony Kushner's *Angels in America,* mentioned in an

If you drive to the show and bring with you only gas money and a beer and some CDs to listen to in the car and on the way you get a phone call talk about nothing and then the show is alright but they don't jam out the Tweezer like you'd like and then afterward the traffic's not bad and you're home from Worcester by a barely past midnight, OK, that's one way, but if you drive out in afternoon light and there are so many blue Fiats on the road that you find your faith in stochasticity not breaking, not yet, but given now an arrhythmic *sway* that might prefigure a (your) Fall…and clouds don't quite part as they should given the forecast (more faith harried more) nor can you shake the memory of a phrase you heard the other day, or was it twenty years ago after a left-not-as-usual-right turn at the front door of the Prendergast Library – *the Dark is Rising* it was, and since then when the light fades wrongly right (or night's longing lingers lightly in light) it is Rising indeed – was it then? was that still you, fore shadow? – on such a greygloom failure of day amidst unrandom assortments of Fiats (blue like crying), *Fiats fuck's sake,* mightn't you bring with you into the warming dark of the theatre a little great something made of magic? And mightn't it play along with and into the music, which too Rises, which bears you up with it? What if up was oceanfloor currents and another open question? What if down were a river of fire within the stone, water stretching as delicate skin all around, broken by bone teeth with mountain shapes?

Couldn't that story be part of the music too? (Don't you wanna go?)

But back down the quieting side it's true, yes, that the right

---

earlier essay, puts this idea to haunting use; in quite another register, the phrase is spoken by the murderous cyborg Roy Batty in the film *Blade Runner,* with Batty in the role of Jacob, with more than a bit of Jesus thrown in for semiotic flavour.

thing is to expect and demand nothing; to give the music every chance to achieve itself. Maybe meditate in the parking lot to keep your vibes right, uncouple zig and zag. At the very least shut up please about how they didn't jam out Tweezer *again* because for a few seconds in the Stash to close the first set they got into this intensely aggressive polytonal wrestle, you might even say a fine ol' donnybrook, this like *contretemps* even like *wow*, Trey was saying F#m and Page reasonably felt B/F but Mike, Mike, trustworthy Michael Gordon would not be derailed from what I can't help thinking was actually a Bb-Ab train of, if not thought then, well, then maybe an actual train…

You can 'think' 'one thing' and that's perfect; or you can try to bring two or three or all the things into collision, that's perfectly fine; fine; that's up to you and your Gods. But surely we're allowed and even encouraged to make a value judgment here to so I'll say the important thing is to stay there as long as you can, and not place your/his/my/her experience of radical simplicity (psychedelia of hysterically present egoless one-only-ness, vast whiteness so empty it fills you lightly) against her/his/your/my experience of radical multiplicity (each arm of the body a body again, equations are cities, light is sound you can taste, each line contains all points (the five Postulates form a Pentagraph), believe as you please but please give it away to the moment). Because **NO,** you're not allowed to hold up your cognition as some holy thing, inerrant, or even benignly neglected by godstochasm, you're not allowed to say *my thoughts are precious* and then like some kind of shitscared teenager *run away* from the demand that that implies, to give this precious thing up to chance, to say that there are better and worse ways of treating yourself but one way of thinking is as good as another; if your thoughts matter and mean then don't back down the minute they threaten to make a universe. At the well-worn point where you habitually turn away to say GOOD BAD WHATEVER, the crook and break that habit's left of you, *that's* where you can salvage even your impure experience of the show, it takes *almost nothing* from you, nothing but It Is What It Is and it's OK that we don't know what to 'make of it.'

Enlightenment won't be austerity. Just being.

You know where Adam and Eve went wrong, what got them into trouble with Dad's Voice?

Editorializing. 'This is the best version of YEM. *Fact.*'

♥ ☞ ✽ ☞ ✼

I guess I'm saying you have to work with what you bring, emotionally, 'spiritually,' medically, intellectually – and all of these are subsumed, you must believe me, by the word 'physically' – and it's OK if your experience is 'impure' or whatever; certainly *imperfect*. It's got to be that way, because *you've* got to be that way. But when you remove your self from a position of judgment upon your own doing, when you (or I!) begin to experience even the 'mediocre' shows as a blessing, offering the same opportunity for (let's call it) true being as 'classic' moments or indeed crapshows, then you (I) don't actually need to play 'best of' games in order to be *safe*. We keep each other safe. Even the nonideal is safe; good thing too, because into that category falls everything that has been or ever will be or trivially coincidentally irrelevantly invisibly miraculously *is*.

> The Blessing gives more life, awards a time without boundaries, and makes a name into a pragmatic immortality, by way of communal memory. Indeed, the Blessing in J cannot be distinguished from the work of memory. (Harold Bloom, *The Book of J*)

DECEMBER 5, CLEVELAND

I: Ghost > Wilson > Bitch > BEK, Sparkle, Jim > My Friend, Ginseng, Limb, Char0 **II:** Stash, Bouncin', Julius > Slave > Lizards, Loving Cup > Chalkdust **E:** Bold as Love

But on the other hand *fuck* this show, know what I'm saying? There's nothing worse in the whole universe than 'nothing special' when you're looking for a fix and this show, as good as it is by any measure a sane person might devise, is nothing special all the same. Fuck too whoever wrote the previous 4,000 words, about wanting to withhold value judgments and refuse the ranking game and just be 'in the moment' whatever that means. (Seriously where else are you gonna be? is it now or not?!) The best-known feature of the show is a 17-minute Julius that really is just that, 17 minutes of Julius, like they really do just *keep playing the song* for a very long time and don't really go anywhere with it, which is just the wooooooooooorst because more than anything I really wanted to open up a 17-minute version of a song not generally treated as a 'jam vehicle' and be, like, blown away by untrammeled creativity and emotional expressivity and whatever I've been going on about this whole time. The woooooorst!!

Disappointment is the most accurate guide to the worth of things, *as I hope I've made clear.*

♥ ☞ ♣ ☞ ✽

The highlight of this Cleveland show, meanwhile, is an absolutely wild version of Slave to the Traffic Light. Slave is normally a *monotonic* climb ('steadily increasing without ever decreasing') to a Trademark Phish Peak, complete with standardized phrasing from Trey in the fashion of Taste and Reba (among other monotonic hush-roar trips). This performance, on the other hand, is both 'unfinished'[58] and quite unusual as versions of Slave go, with Fish's seemingly inappropriate doubletime beat lifting the rest of the band outta the sometimes torpid Slave mood and into an extraordinary stadium-anthem jam, complete with more Jimi licks from Trey and bludgeoning two-note bass figures from Mike (Page done the reqwyrt then too, smashing hell out of the piano like a good man should). For a long while in there it doesn't quite sound like Slave, or rather it sounds like Trey's doppelgänger is playing Slave while Trey hisownself wails away up top with the other guys' help to try and scare the creature off, which they do eventually, along with everyone else in the city of Cleveland.

I'm writing about these shows largely in chronological order, a different show every few days, and it's hard for me to get too worked up about this genuinely excellent show, knowing what happens tomorrow – tomorrow-then, I mean. The 6th. The Palace. Well: Trey shows up weirdly late for the atmospheric Ghost opener but makes up for it with a ferocious Jim, and there's a wonderfully knotty segue into My Friend My Friend (one of Trey's more impressive short-form compositions I think); lead duties on Limb by Limb seem to be more democratically shared than usual, for a time anyway, resulting in a dense performance without the ejaculatory finish that marks the best-known versions (think 6/19/04). Stash is up to snuff for 1997, which is to say it's seamless, effortless, a showpiece tune for a band that was then fully finally able to grasp simplicity amidst complexity, seemingly at will; Chalkdust is at its blistering best, joyfully adolescent as it nearly falls apart – as it should be. Damn! What-

---

[58] (like a birthday candle that gutters and vanishes from being unwatched, with no happy grade schooler's breath to snuff it out before time's time)

ever.

There's only so much to say here. This is a good strong show with a moody, intense second set. They are a very talented band and this is the sort of thing they did, back then, every single night, modulo the occasional serious chemical impairment or goofoff interlude. I feel (and take great pleasure in) a twilit shroomy continuity between Ghost, Katy, Jim, Stash, and especially the Julius > Slave pairing; the whole show feels like a holistic creation, that extraordinary quality Fall 97 tended to have, and the extravagant Liz/Cup/Chalk run to end the show is both totally self indulgent and justified, the band have more than earned the right to just wail away happily for twenty-odd minutes after surviving hostile terrain and harsh elements in Stash/Julius/Slave.

I think I'm content to leave the Cleveland show as I find it: as the necessary sunsetting, the sacrificial invocation, between the warm glow of the Philly shows on one temporal side and Attainment on the other. I don't know what to make of it, Reader(s). I'm genuinely sorry. It's just *really good*. There's nothing worse than that in the whole world.

clearing

I wrote this for V's birthday in October 2008. It's how I think of change.

All of us at outer edges grow without growing, more space upon but same within, endless bounded change, sides splitting, lines interposed amid lines. Language of new skin and surface. Each learned gesture or word of us offers a new subidentity: arc becomes wave, tooth becomes star, a geography of notions and remembrance. New map embraces new world. Our outer edge curls back and turns outward, the evolutionary arc of You; and heart's reach lies within unknowable borders, a catastrophe of repetitious yes, segments opening like arms to keep outside out. The derived folds and distractions of skin, a thicket lying in lines. The sweep of time and body knows no direction nor scale, only shape: onward is in and around, eversoftening perimeter of the self in a circle, inlets and secret harbours, tonight the salty crook of elbow, tomorrow an errant fingertip, the next day the imaginary march of cells. Enumerated currents. Each region of segmented space its children's template, grand growing family, and at arm's length or numeric remove the great shape of us is apparent. The fractal scape of You. A pageant of complexity: and time is our author and our home. We stage the variegating drama for its benefit, and it flows unceasing for ours, each's eyes on the other. Strands of something: the sighing helices of friends, loves, selves. We twist and splinter and recombine like stories. Time to us an arrow - and to time, the outer edges of us an endless pathway, each place a movement, each new border an event. A line interlocking its forebears. At arm's length we might see: the ongoing tale of meaningless years. Yes, and matched curls and lines, invitations, hearts, the swell and recess of music, the gasp of nearness, letterforms one by one emerging, every variation of the first form, record of its own birth. Yes: and the outline of wings, or newborn light. Rising.

♥ ☞ ✤ ☞ ✳

I wrote this for myself in April 2010. It's how I think of love.

We must tell you. We speak for nonsense, for emptiness, for transformation by wild caprice, for water and fire and wind, for the crackling desiccation that is autumn, the flood and onrush of springtime renaissance. We wish for the heat and nakedness of summer, wash, bray, collapse, caress, great bottles of dry spirits poured haphazardly into upturned mouths and over skin. We exult in the salt spray of the sea and the percussive snap of the forest floor amid autumn's diminuendo. We ask for no permission and brook no certainty or stricture. We lie still as tide pools. We fuck when we please and savour the quiet that follows a day's dedicated work. Our lips taste of wine and the metallic tang of summer sweat is at our throats. We speak unfamiliar thoughts and dance complex figures that exist only in the tap of toes this very instant or the tip trace of questioning fingers. We have this and there is nothing else. We claim no souls and honour the continuity of circumstance. We love catastrophically, ecstatically, thoughtfully, delicately, heroically. We love in the musical language that a hundred billion years ago birthed and culminated unimaginable universes where the name of light could be freely spoken. We create love in abundance. We fall away ceaselessly from present to memory and dismiss every possible future. We dream one another and each of us is a dream's momentary form. We are the secret the music reveals. Watch the pattern the silence weaves as we depart, listen carefully to the colours that constitute each earthly form, trust in the joining of hands and the riotous music of rainfall. Here we are in a language that can only be called love at a moment that must always become love for a purpose that can never surpass love, and we are given by the great accident of time no recourse but to one another. The creation is ongoing. The rapture is ongoing. Shadows coil, gather, coolly recur, and what seems the cycle of seasons is a trick of perspective. We drink to the instant of spring, the notion of summer, the illusion of winter, the possibility of autumn. Lift up voices, meet eyes, link hands, and joyfully listen. We are the promise that laughter fulfills. There is nothing to us but one another. We are given to create and to grant, to revolve, to gather and to detonate, to consider, to sing, to go on and on forever in unimaginable forms. Amen. It is given to us only to love to be loved and to be love and all and each is every other, amen, we love you, we love, we are love, amen.

❤ ☞ ✤ ☞ ✻

I wrote this for myself in June 2010. It's how I think of human beings.

Somebody's brother loves somebody else's; kid in a coffee shop remembers a killing field and the smell of dead nameless children; the noise of the city is overcome by stillness, not forever; some well-meaning young wife's mighty efforts on love's behalf prove inadequate. A schoolteacher waves dismissal, insists she'll eat tomorrow, it's OK, tomorrow, but her cheer is unconvincing. A veteran retreats after refusing to beg for a job, but only just, and the door of the community center bangs his elbow. She thinks to herself C'mon we can't help everybody but says to him Maybe next month. Jogging hurts after so many months off and he mulls over turning around (but she likes him thin). She holds her breath watching the church doors, waiting though she can't say for what, and behold: no one comes out or says Welcome, we've been waiting too; she can't stay, can't go, can't make her way in. An hour after quitting his job at the used bookstore he calls her Kind of clumsy, you know? In front of a friend thinking she'll laugh and roll her eyes and laugh like she always does and be forever and ever his to do as he will, he loves her laugh, but this time she doesn't. Their shame is not play-acting this time. Somebody's ex-husband misses some ex-wife's broad shoulders; baby under the folds of a loose gathered blanket murmurs and passes and will be mourned; some smartly-appointed young fellow grandly gives up his cab for some smoldering account executive, she doesn't say thank you, he mutters Bitch and his surprise isn't quite believable. Neither is yours. A nasty preconception is confirmed by a quick glance over her shoulder: gossip magazine. He thinks it's appendicitis but it's gas, but won't always be. The feeder road looks like a river from up here, and the river is invisible. He doesn't like to think of himself as taking advantage. She had a perfect ass but was preoccupied with her work so he left. He talked a decent game but kept mentioning her body so she checked out, silently, hours before. The kind of graduate student who still gets pimples uses phrases like The wretched of the earth and his website hasn't been updated in a while. She misses her scent. Grandly he says I have very simple tastes. The work piles up on the desk by the exterior wall; the bicycle isn't going to fix itself; chicks who play the drums like that can get away with being mean, am I right? Somebody's mentor has a moment of irresponsibility and it costs them both incalculably, invisibly; the one father in the new parents group seems a little defensive; she realizes she wasn't picked last this time; she doesn't think It's complicated is actually a good defense for all his racist attitudes, even at his age. Her way of criticizing gently. His unguardedness. He tries to be comforting but she's learned to deal with it and doesn't need to be protected any more. No room in there for losers, kiddo. The hottest day of the summer they crowd into the bar anyway and order ice water in plastic cups, shed layers, rub melting ice upon bared secret skin. The music is perfect you can't even hear the music we are the music as it is made. Everything is; the map has no edges; somebody's story is somebody else's sister; he says quietly, finally, I feel alone; every possible world is inevitable and somewhere in the city somebody steps with delicious hesitancy from one, now, to the next, there, and onward, listen, and meaninglessly onward, yes.

and furthermore

DECEMBER 6, AUBURN HILLS

I: Golgi, Antelope, Train Song, Gin > Foam, Sample, Fee, Maze, Cavern **II:** Tweezer > Izabella > Twist > Piper > Sleeping Monkey > Tweeprise **E:** Rocky Top

The first thing to say, I've already said, in a comment at 'Mr Miner's Phish Thoughts,' *phishthoughts.com,* in incredulous response to another comment, quoted below, by a poster named 'Wilson' or something. Wilson, it seemed, had never yet heard this show.

How is that even *possible.*

```
"Listened to that '97 Auburn Hills show for the
first time last night. Not even sure what to say.
It's astounding."
```

ARE YOU FUCKING KIDDING ME

dogg pay attention now,

IN THE BEGINNING the universe was created.
mistake.

fast forward 6,000 years
tray is up at a party jamming for twelve days
straight on "mcgriff the faithful hosedog" or
whatever

flashman comes up and is like DOGG I PLAY DRUMS
tray is like LKADJSF;LKAJSD;FKLAJSD;LKFJASD;LFJK

they form a band called PHLASH

they get larry page and gordon ramsay to play
washboard
and brass
respectively

now, like conjoined twins at the beach,

THEY ARE IN A FOUR-PIECE

attention

flashman is like RED ROVER WHY ARE WE HERE

gordon is like ALLO WOTCHER CUNTS
and larry page is too busy building database-
backed websites to even give a fuck

he can only spare one hand to play solos
because the other hand is stroking his
million-mile-high pile of

LOOT

attention wilson are you fucking listening to
this part

TRAY LOOKS AT GOD DAMN FLASHMAN WITH PITY
flashman is like WE GOT THIS 4 PIECE

tray is like LKAJ;DSLFKJASDF ;,MNZXCV,MNXC,MV

flashman is like IF YOU DONT TELL ME WHAT THE
FUCK TO DO RIGHT THE FUCK NOW I WILL NEVER TELL
YOU WHERE I KEEP THE PLEASURE ANIMALS

and

tray is like ON 12-6-97 IN THE VERY BUILDING
WHERE THE CLIMAX OF ROBOCOP FUCKING TAKES PLACE,
SHIT WILL BECOME CLEAR LIKE A CHANDELIER

he is adamant

......

fast forward another 6,000 years

it is 12-6-97

fucking PHLASH play the single greatest shit they've ever played

it is so intense it isn't even music anymore at one point emily dickinson is fucking soloing on the vacuum cleaner

backstage

and that's only the 955th most unlikely thing happening

emily is a beast on the hard bop tunes you have no idea

WILSON LISTEN THIS IS THE END PART

BIG FINISH

fast forward 65 million years to last night you listened to the - what the fuck did i call it - "SINGLE GREATEST BALLISTIC COCK-MISSILE EVER FIRED FROM THE GROIN OF A ROCK BAND INTO THE WAITING FUCK-EARS OF AMERICA"

and, LO, tray's prophesies didst come to pass

```
and, LO, it was good
```

```
haters gonna hate though
```

I've changed 'Siamese' to 'conjoined' since originally posting it; as my wife was forced to remind me, you can only get away with so much 'ironic' racism, specifically *zero,* before it becomes pathetic/vile. But I've left in the 'ballistic cock missile' stuff, which I like even less. Well, what can I say. In a boys' club, that's the language – and Phish fandom is a boys' club.[59]

♥ ☞ ✤ ☞ ✻

The music is purple, or the sound is.

I have strong colour-senses associated with some musics, for whatever reason. 6/17/94 is green. 2/28/03 is blue. The Went is yellow/green – chromatic open space. 2/20/93 is blue/black on white. Sometimes my old j-cards (cassette tape paper inserts) overdetermine my memory: 12/14/95 is dark yellow-orange, the Fleezer is alien green, 2/17/97 royal blue, but those are easy to explain.

Mysteriously, 12/6/97 is purple – the rich purple of Kuroda's lights, specifically, like bioluminescent morning glories.

In college I used to listen to the second set of this show over and over along with 12/30, 7/2, 2/17 (all 1997 – peak fandom), 12/14/95, 8/20/93…the transition from Izabella into Twist, via that riotous dance-funk interlude, was perfect music to me. I'd turn off my bedroom lights, crank up the stereo, maybe lie on

---

[59] I'm not aware of even a single woman who posts regularly to the phish.net – at least I can't recall any woman explicitly identifying herself as such on the site. Certainly there are female fans, even hardcore tour rats, but online fandom is for guys to talk to one another. Ever wonder why the Internet sucks? That's a big part of why the Internet sucks.

the couch or just lean waaaaaay back in my desk chair, and suddenly I'd be surrounded by deep purple light. This happens to me surprisingly often – the mild synesthesia I spoke of earlier. It's not interesting in itself, really; I mention it only as a maybe-silly example of how anyone's private experience of the music has more to do with her or his weird cognitive predispositions than with any formal feature of the music itself. Which isn't to say there's nothing to be gained from formal study – Trey's own skill is proof of that, if any were needed – but rather that when I go on about this show, my barely-hidden real subject is my experience of my Self, as the music mirrors it (me) back to me.

When the Palace show saw official release – on just a couple weeks' public notice, if I remember correctly! – I ran out and grabbed it just like every other dweeb. This is my deathbed request soundboard, for heaven's sake, the one show I'd *needed* a perfect[60] recording of since the very first time I heard it, presumably in early '98. And there it was: my single favourite Phish performance ready to explode from my silicone-tipped earbuds directly into my brainheart.

It was a huge disappointment.

♥ ☞ ♣ ☞ ✻

Even in the context of Fall 97, the December 6th show is a standout performance. Phish only played Gin three times during the whole tour, twice in an early first-set slot, and on both those occasions the band glided smoothly from the rickety, *square* rhythms of the song proper to a bright easy climax – then segued equally

---

[60]'Needed' and 'perfect' should be in gigantic neon-lit scare quotes, for reasons that damned well ought to be obvious to any thinking adult – 'needed' in particular. I've written about that stuff, the misperception of desire as need (and the difference between intratextual and metatextual desire), at extraordinary length here: http://waxbanks.typepad.com/blog/2007/03/what_you_want_w.html.

smoothly into another old tune, like slipping into a well-worn pair of shoes. In Champaign it was Gin > Llama; here it's a more textural Gin jam, with Trey trilling away at the third as in a Fall 97 Hood (or the magnificent 12/31/10 Ghost), and a diabolical segue into Foam. Maze runs to fully 15 minutes, one of those wild jams where everyone in the band is moving so fast that their flittering microrhythms cancel each other out, and what's left is steady harmonic oscillation, so many notes per second that only a seismic movement is discernible through the din. Even Antelope, the first real hitter of the show, gets extra mustard – before Trey begins his steady ascent into mania there's fully four minutes of eerie delay loops, coolly swinging dance rhythms, and what the kidz today call 'swank' clav-groove dorkistry from the Humbert Humbert of the clavinet, Mr Page McConnell. Antelope goes nearly 17 minutes without overstaying its welcome – compare, if you like, to the Hampton openers.

It's just a dead solid first set, with three jams worth seeking out and a bonus performance of Mike's creepy little miniature, Train Song.[61]

And then there's the second set. It's…a tower: one continuous performance that just reaches higher and digs deeper and gets more and more compact and intense and dreamlike as it goes. It's got one of the all-time great Tweezers, in which the gnarliest Tweezfunk of the month morphs improbably into a soul-shredding guitar chorale with an underlying six-beat feel

---

[61]Aah, Train Song. I sang that tune *a cappella* for a high school jazz chorus audition. The next year I think I did the opening section of Bohemian Rhapsody. One year I auditioned wearing Erin S.'s 'hippie' skirt. I was a nerdy kid and didn't feel comfortable everywhere I went, even at school where I tended to be on good terms with the faculty, but I was *totally* at home in the school music suite. Now I write for a living, more or less, and am decent at it; but for comfort I come here, to write for (to be with) you. And this music. Nothing changes except everything.

and a restlessly shifting drum line from Fishman. There are elements of the Fall 97 'space jams' in the post-Tweezer incantation, but to a much greater degree than on (say) 11/14 or 11/22, the entire band is in freedom flight here – the guitar is the lead voice but there's none of the ol' 'that man Keaton seems to be the whole show' stuff…

And the segue into Izabella is perfect and coming out of it they hit on a devastating dance groove,

riding Fish's woodblock ticktock down a series of two-man groove breaks to an eerie Twist whose written arrangement is studded with funky guitar/keys work but whose jam crests early

and then

c'mon

dissolves into hushed whispers and the gentle opening to Piper,

which just builds and builds to an unexpected hybrid jam somewhere in the haunted triangle defined by the eerie quiet of the Twist outro,

c'mon this is too easy

the cannonball momentum of Izabella,

and the stately crescendo that gives shape to Piper itself, but you know all this already because you're well over a hundred pages into a book about a single rock band's 1997 Fall Tour and how could you *not?* but if you don't then read on, but then hold on wait, because I have to pull up hard on the reins (haven't even mentioned Sleeping Monkey) (*so what*) because,

as I heard myself say,

'huge disappointment'

❤ ☞ ❀ ☞ ✻

The sound is purple, whatever the music is. Whatever they *were*.

My old audience recording of the show was, as they say, 'of unknown lineage.' The 'generation' of a live Phish tape is the number of times it's undergone *lossy transfer*. For instance:

microphone > DAT > cassette > cassette

is known as a DAUD-2, i.e. Digital source, 2 **AUD**ience generations.

Probably I should've mentioned this on like page 4.

Copying from DAT to DAT, or DAT to WAV/FLAC file on your computer, preserves all the information in the original recording. Dubbing to cassette tape means losing a little something (and introducing hiss). Too many cassette generations and a tape becomes unlistenable – no one likes a DAUD-3, though hell I've had (treasured!) DAUD-5's.

The sound matters.

Soundboard recordings capture only (or almost solely) the instruments themselves – some audience noise sneaks into the vocal mics and there might be a crowd mic to provide a bit of ambience, but you don't hear the instruments as they sound in the room; you hear the raw material, the sound emerging directly from the instruments. Fishman's drums don't echo; Trey's guitar hasn't searched the space and returned transformed; Mike's bass hasn't yet resonated throughout the venue structure; and while Page's keyboards are actually audible,[62] they haven't yet taken the shape of the crowd, his piano strings haven't yet caught and refracted the sound of the other instruments.

What a soundboard recording offers is clarity; what it loses is atmosphere, the sense of the Event – and crucially, of the

---

[62] The piano is the bane of Phish's audience tapers. The Dead's too, as I recall – it's damn hard to hear Keith on so many of those AUDs from the 1970s. Blame the sound guys, in part, for featuring Garcia/Anastasio above all else.

thousands of people present, whose audible energy is such an important element of the band's experience, and the course of the show in turn. A well-made matrix recording, which mixes multiple sources (usually a SBD/AUD blend), offers the best of both worlds: a clear representation of what the musicians are actually *doing* onstage, rendered in all the wild unpredictable colours which the sound takes on in the room, and with the audience's every cheer or moan or whisper caught too. The message and the meaning all at once.

Recent official *livephish.com* releases have tended to be very, very light on audience noise – and offer little of the feel of the rooms they were recorded in. They're recordings of and by and for machines, quite different from the nearly human listening-in that AUDs offer. The 12/6/97 LivePhish release, which is (to be clear) *a treasure,* fits this pattern. To take the clearest example, the guitar sound that everyone heard, including the musicians, wasn't the pure waveform coming from the guitar itself, but the movement of smoke and fog produced by enormous speaker stacks right in the room; but this album captures what Trey *meant* rather than what he actually said, without the cavernous darkness that makes AUD recordings of the 12/6 show (and indeed the whole tour) so special. This isn't four guys; it's four instruments.

In January 1998 I brought my tape deck to a 'listening party' at David R.'s apartment in Porter Square. A bunch of local fans gathered. There were four or five other decks there; we daisy-chained them and made, at one stroke, five or six second-generation copies of somebody's delicious audience recording of 12/30/97 – a show that'd taken place just a couple of weeks before. The effects of THC were enjoyed, your humble author got his first exposure to *Live/Evil,* laughter and camaraderie were shared, and it was one of the best days out I'd had in, maybe, my life 'til then. Certainly in college. I haven't felt part of the Phish-fan tribe in many, many years, but that afternoon I certainly did.

The tape in question, my precious DAUD–2, became my sonic template for the Fall. The winged rush of Fish's ghost notes on the snare; cascade of guitar haze, like a fall of stardust, that gave Trey's 'space jam' solo statements their unique feel; the way Page's Rhodes keyboard would wrap around the rhythm bed, binding up the ensemble sound for the guitar to lift up into some barely-visible Upper realm; and of course Mike's new ass-smack attack on the bass, which could sound almost ironic-apologetic in his upper register but called down bodily apocalypse when he hammered his low strings. It's *supposed* to sound like that; that's the True Name of the music, its presentation in the moment…

…assuming, of course, an audience tape can capture even the *faintest hint* of the actual experience of that place and time…

…which is a whole other story, a sore spot in the community for many years, which flashes regularly into tiresome online shouting/pissing matches between those who write about live recordings on their own terms (e.g. me), and those who insist that the tapes are just photographs of a living thing, and have none of the same life themselves – mnemonics at best. It's not really an argument, to be frank; the tapes (mp3's) exist for everyone, but the moment is gone, so it's good to talk about the tapes since they'll be around in ten or twenty years when the next buncha kids goes looking for 'that band my parents were into in college, Fish or something…'

Oh man, I'm listening to it now, and it's *really* embarrassing that Trey can't remember the lyrics to Izabella, the only weak spot in an otherwise blissfully unhinged performance. C'mon, man! It's not like it's three verses of blues *total* or anything, ya fuckin' *stoner.*

♥ ☞ ✤ ☞ ✻

Apocalyptic time. Private narrative time. Time as a series of postures of receptivity – instead of years, entries or refusals. Instead of nights, Shows. I can't come to the music new, and its power to make us new isn't limitless; my next listen is always the next chapter in an ongoing private story.

The official release of the Palace show disappointed me, and I found myself actually experiencing the music itself for the first time, which was joyful and new, but worrying too. (*There's* a bundle of contradictions, if you like.) For one thing, this is the Best Set Phish Ever Played, the purest essence – but I can now think *offhand* of three or four sets, already discussed herein, that are 'better.'[63] More to the point, it's My Favourite Set, which is to say one of my favourite musical anythings, but my experience of it until now was never – or I guess only once was, the very first time – well it hasn't ever been a 'purely musical' experience. There was always some degree of fulfillment or refusal, which could only be expressed in terms of my own weird (but decidedly not Weird) expectations. My Favourite Set was always about my *idea* of the perfect set; the Best Set Phish Ever Played is nothing more an expression of my ideals – or worse, my *habits*. (You just

---

[63]In fact, they might've played better sets in the last two years, whatever 'better' means. If 8/19/12 Set Two had happened when Phish were the biggest touring band in America, instead of an inescapably 'retro' act (however forward-looking their current music), we'd be talking about it as one of the all-time greats. But no one's paying attention now. Of course, the band stuck around after the fireworks on that night – the center of the show, 53 minutes of perfect improv, constitutes just the first *half* of the set! In 1997 they coulda just walked offstage after Theme, or else played YEM right then for the clincher. But there's more than 20 minutes of largely pointless filler between those two tunes. Oh well.

can't (afford to) be principled in a pissing contest.)

Which isn't to say this performance isn't impressive in itself – plenty of other people count it among their all-time favourites, and while it's poor form to hide out in the majority in such matters, the appeal of this set, particularly its stunning first half-hour, should be clear even to non-fans. Come to it a virgin: that's a righteous bit of funk to start things off, the band obviously 100% in sync from the first note, and the evolution of Tweezer's dance-floofery into a grand guitar hymn really is one of the most patient, empathetic improvisations of Phish's career (and patient empathetic improv is their specialty, so that's saying something). This is tight-loose playing of the highest order; there are no technical obstacles between the band's emotions and their expression, and they're all so comfortable with their roles (particularly at this point late in a year of transformation) that there's no interpersonal friction to overcome either, no ego. This is the Big Idea: mere communication. Communion. The Hampton Halley's is the same sort of performance, but this is the Platonic essence realized: total internal fluidity, perfect outer form.

Still, it's not complete without what comes immediately after, broadening path down from the peak into heavy growth soaking sweat and muscles hammering angry way through to that thrash. Izabella, damn. Lucky they're in the right key or else more (or much less I guess) than lucky. When Page's left hand joins in on that mighty riff and everyone in the room is hollering and sorry but *control has definitely been lost,* that's the demon the conjurer calls to every night and here she is. Dark as damn and bloodthirsty. (*'The world moves on a woman's hips /the world moves and it bounces and hops...'*) Fishman's breaking up the bigger beat by shifting measures, 2 to 3 to 4 to 6 and now hammering imposition of fours upon threes and the rhythms's happening (hard-beat hammering body's a cage) before the idea of the next tune has quite coalesced – it's like Fish and Trey are racing together toward the next song to almost the same under innerscore and they arrive at the falls together ('I can't swim!' 'Are you crazy? The *fall* will probably kill you')…even two beats out of phase they make a perfect pair here. That's the miracle's name: much more than coincidence, they're happening here on a genuine unity of thought and feeling. Everyone onstage is feeling the same thing, and because they're working so hard (as professional moment-makers) to let a shared emotional impulse dictate their actions, the tumble from scherzophrenic phase-shifting guitar helices to funky-bluesy guerrilla wah is seamless and seemingly inevitable.

But 'seemingly inevitable' is *my* call, innit. Don't tend to call things *inevitable* until after the fact (the fall); 'it could never have been otherwise' is a lot easier than 'it's gonna go down this way.' Which anyway the minute you stop for such *pronunciamenti* the music's dead, you're asking folks to notice you instead of being with/in them, being for something, getting small to make room for the music…

The very best part of the set, I've always insisted, is the dance riot that spins out of the Izabella. There's a creepy-old-church version of Twist to come, and a storm to try and outrun in Piper (you can't) (caught is bliss); not to mention Sleeping Monkey in defiance of sense or taste; but for five minutes between Trey's switch to chicken-scratch rhythm work outtabella and the drum-bass touchdown right into Twist, they're lost to body logic – bliss is to close your eyes and follow the great curve and they do, full five minutes they enter the beat of some hidden heart.

No technique here. Like degree of technical difficulty *zero*. The judges are bored stiff.

But the line's unbroken. How often does that ever happen. Bloodline, lifeline, straight through from one moment to the next without so much as a stutter.

You're following the line too, trusting. That's one of the great gifts that honest art can give: permission to be trusting, to recognize our connection to the greater organism. Feel your bones fusing to the superstructure. Share your blood. Conjoin.

> as he saw his life run away from him
> thousands ran along
> chanting words to a song:
>
> please me have no regrets
> came from the baby's mouth.
>
> we follow the lines going south.
> –Marc Daubert, 'The Curtain'

Ley lines, blazed trails through old forest, blood of a great beast; crowds shout, time gathers; he gets old and old thoughts come in a young voice. A song. No regrets.

I don't *think* that's good poetry but there's something about it: feels like motes of light stolen each from one of many worlds, glowing together in loose form. Several forms within. 'We follow the lines going south': a billion or more stories you could steal that line from. Thousands ran; words to a song; image of plenty and of a single line (ahem) passing between the many bodies (make a macrobody). Most of Phish's lyrics are bullshit but somehow these lines (ahem) thread still through me. How I think my self, my *many*, into coherence.

The music is purple and The Curtain wasn't actually played at this show; I had an atrial fibrillation that lasted six hours, an electrical dysfunction caused a skip in the rhythm of my poor heart; for six hours I thought I would surely die, that my heart was dying already, that I'd failed, would leave my son and wife alone in the world without my (ha) help (haha)…they say you don't really have to worry until the second day, when the inefficiency of your heart's stutter puts you at risk of a stroke, blood pools within your upper chambers, you *must not stand still.* When steady rhythm is restored they say you've 'converted to sinus' but what they mean is *breathe again.* Your son's daddy won't die today. Absolute terror for weeks, then right back to whatever screwups I was getting into before death dreams distracted me. Sitting around listening to Phish probably. Keep a steady pulse day to day.

A purely private experience. This is how I think (of) myself. How humans bring the ideas of themselves into physical being, into action: you become what you *love.* Owners look like their dogs, or the other way 'round; your accent changes and words you borrow from even this adopted place; your heart learns its rhythm from your nearby mother's heart, the mechanism of love, deep feeling (feeling erupts desperately deep); or she goes and you forget and your heart, the rhythm you do, it *breaks…*

Here's a little thing: this is my *favourite show,* which when you've heard so many shows is 'kind of a big deal' as the kidz say. But 'favourite' *isn't actually a comparison* when you get down to it; it just means that, say, you like orange juice better than apple, apple better better than prune, but then there's this drink called *bourbon* which you (1) *don't* actually want to drink all the time, indeed probably don't drink as often as fruit juice, but which (2) occupies this special place in your heart the way the clunky Curtain lyrics have stayed with me even as I've lost the specifics of, say, Penn Warren's 'Audubon' (which isn't just 'better,' it's as good as anything I know, yet still 'not my favourite,' *gaaaah* this is needlessly complicated)...

My desire to talk about *Tweezer > Izabella > Twist > Piper* isn't motivated by some notion that you, Reader(s), would benefit from my think-by-think recap; I'm not talking through my favourite set because it's great, I'm sharing my pleasure in this music, and the *sharing* is a big part of what 'favourite' actually means – it's the outward face of my love for the music, the measure I abide by. What's yours? NYE 95? 11/11/73? *In a Silent Way? Exile in Guyville? In the Wee Small Hours?* There's no way you could possibly compare these things. (The phrase 'best sex I ever had' is a little crazy too; if you're not willing to tell future lovers they can never measure up, that you're settling and 'happy with what you've got' but nothing can touch those memories, then you *seriously* need to let go of that stupid ranking bullshit and start doing right by other human beings instead of kneeling for ghosts...)

The best show is the next one; it's the chance you take. That should tell you something about your 'favourites,' and I bet we're all quite grownup enough to...to...

Aah to hell with it. All this aspirational talk of egolessness and no longer acting like a (bunch of) teenager(s) is nice but we both know this whole book falls into the crack between the keys: we wanna get to the next thing purely awake and wanting but it's hard not to retreat into the old thing, the edifice of self.

As long as I define myself by my favourite pop culture bitsies, I'm choosing to remain a child. Not 'childlike': a child. A *putz*.

'What is love? One name for it is knowledge.'

So making love is learning. *Learning is making love.*

Free your favourite.[64]

♥ ☞ ♣ ☞ ✳

So maybe 12/2 II is a better set, and maybe you'll never recapture the feeling of first love (don't say 'true love,' this is grownup business), but so what.

Fishman announces the end of each Reba's jam segment with four beats of downhill rolling tom-toms. You never wanna hear those signal drums; they're the counterspell, they wish away the glorious Lydian surround. But some of that composition's power comes from its *pitilessness,* the threat of having our fun taken away. 'Great stories end' isn't always precisely true, but dramatic shape is a strong mnemonic device; stories that end are able to stay with us – they fit our wishing. When crusty Phish fans talk about how the glory days of Reba and Hood are largely past, that's *part* of what they mean: the beauty of inner worlds that rest in memory, held guiltlessly (can you blame them?) against the beauty of the world yet to be revealed. (The glory days are: tomorrow. That's the Blessing, right?)

I could use some of that right here. Not that we've risen into bliss or anything – but we gotta get to the whistling part. This one's got to end somehow—

DECEMBER 7, DAYTON

I: Bag > Psycho Killer > Jesus > My Mind > Ice > Swept > Steep > Ice > Theme, Tube, Tube Jam > Slave **II:** Timber > Wolfman's > Boogie > Reba, Guyute > Possum **E:** Day in the Life

---

[64] I don't *think* I mean 'flee'...

DECEMBER 9, PENN STATE

I: Mike's > Chalkdust, My Soul, Stash > H2 > Weekapaug, Dogs Stole, Beauty of My Dreams, Horn > Cup **II:** Julius > Simple > Timber > Contact, Axilla > Hood **E:** Fire

DECEMBER 11, ROCHESTER

I: Punch > Disease > Maze, Dirt, Limb, Cup > Top **II:** Drowned > Roses > Furry > Ghost > Disease > Johnny **E:** Waste

DECEMBER 12 AND 13, ALBANY

I: Bitch > 2001 > Camel, Taste > Bouncin', Tweezer > Train > Char0 **II:** Saw It Again > Piper > Swept > Steep > Caspian > Jam > Izabella, Tweeprise **E:** Guyute, Antelope

I: Ya Mar > Azilla > Theme, Ginseng, Strange Design, Sample, Vulture, Tube, GXBX **II:** NICU > Punch > Ghost > Mike's > Llama, Circus, Weekapaug > Catapult > Weekapaug, Hood **E:** My Soul, Coil

sense of an ending

caffeine kick to a dead horse. thoughts get you going but then chemicals to keep it. keep them too. third floor of the new place with red curtains letting in just a little light. red splash on our high ceiling like church stained windows. there's always abdominal pain lately, abominable, predictable. coffee solo before breakfast, that's what you get. eating slow away at your inner line. if my son could just hug me now to give a new start. new kind of energy. i transmute plants into words by way of an intermediate process of brewing, cooling, pouring over ice. always ice coffee even in winter. avoiding the subject you see. my wife: always hot coffee even in high summer. two of a perfect kind. avoiding the subject.

endings. thinking in china miéville's *kraken*. he's only good looking in his author photo. bit of a dweeb otherwise i think. he carries himself well. you have to when you're eight feet tall and covered with medals, not to mention two dozen piercings in just a single ear, each made of a prehistoric arrowhead, each subtly poisoned, plus you've got a phd in econobollocks or related field…

many endings. 'the ends of the world.' 'end of the world?' '*ends.*' many private times in superposition, shared velocity but private intention, even position…a terrible oneness. or not so bad, i guess, if what you like is just doing stuff with other folks, y'know, just…stuff…

thinking in and around this book. squid cultists – there's your fish/phish connection if you like. not cthulhu, though of course that's one of the not-so-secret referents. playing on the same revulsion while naming away the Name; wanna make your own name, ideally. especially if it's something catchy like 'china.' canny move. anyhow a london full of squid cultists among other genre bits (talking tattoos, squirrels for hire, horny lady cops of course) and everyone, all the nutters and the adepts and sensitives of every sort, they all get not just a feeling but certain knowledge that the world is coming to an end. so many ham-psychic-radio operators can't be wrong. a shared *destination.*

tony soprano asked his shrink if she ever got the sense that she'd come in at the very end of something. i was like *what an old man* but secretly i was exactly what he meant. i'm a sign of his end times. frank sobotka says 'we used to build shit in this country' and i'm the thief he's thinking of, hands in the next guy's pocket. sign he'll die a mere man, time goes on. you are too, probably. (especially if you're reading this on an iPad or something.) apocalyptic fever. the music becomes the time, or vice-versa: 'pre-millennium tension' the man said it was, and after all wouldn't a musician be in a position to know. tricky kid. voice like that. gravel ground. new brokenness, are you into it. into the dust was once your bones.

i don't wanna know i'll die.

but then it isn't death is the problem, not really. buffy dies at the end of season five (sorry spoilers) and it's one of these perfect moments. her gravestone in the final shot: 'SHE SAVED THE WORLD. A LOT.' string section in the score, fade to black, all done. but the show got picked up for two more seasons so they, and she, had to come back. 'have the characters go through what the audience is going through,' the chief writer used to say. instant emotional buy-in. good as the next couple seasons at times were, there was something a little *off* about the show. the arc had finished; what was left? she fought a god in season five, how come the season six villains are literally three nerds in a basement? 'life is the big bad,' the writers said. oh. ('i came back wrong,' buffy said. oh.) (the show is named after her; or she's named after the feeling you get watching, rooting for, *realizing* you're rooting for, a cheerleader killing vampires with kung fu. symbol of the act. 'buffy' is what that shit feels like. what else could you possibly call it or her? 'francine'?)

caffeine worn off. fear now, of not finishing. outrun by chemistry or death, whichever.

in summer 1998 i said goodbye to my mom and brother in new york city and got on a return bus to boston. that was a weekend, i think; maybe i came back on monday or something. they returned to our tiny hometown via other means; maybe mom drove? my girlfriend lived near providence. internship at some floridly-named architectural firm. i went to visit her. did we almost break up that week? well, it was a week. at the weekend i got on a bus to the northern tip of maine to see a rock band. *in march 2009, this is how that felt:*

The band had chartered the buses, a smart move given the awful traffic sure to form at the base's single gate, and tickets for the weekend – two shows, roundtrip bus fare, a place to pitch a tent – came to $150 or something. It was August 1998. I had finished my freshman year of college, had just returned from my first trip to New York City with my family, had prayed in St Patrick's Cathedral, feeling customarily guilty about the usual things. The bus left Boston at something like midnight. I didn't have a tent, hadn't given it any thought, but on the ride up I got to talking with a bearded blonde guy from Providence, another college student, who enthusiastically offered crash space in his tent. It was probably the noisiest bus ride I've ever taken, even counting elementary school trips in Houston, where everything's noisy. The tour rats had presumably made their way to Limestone the same way they'd crossed the country during Summer Tour, so the bus was full of younger kids, college students, the less adventurous sort of fan. The smell of patchouli was of course overwhelming. I'd packed a single shirt for the whole weekend, and no longer remember how much underwear I brought.

On the ride up to Limestone I asked the driver to throw a tape of mine on the stereo, and he obliged. It was a muddy recording of the 7/17 show at the Gorge, recorded just a few weeks prior, having come to me via an informal network of tape traders on the band's unofficial Internet fan newsgroup. It was a DAUD–1 tape, meaning a first-generation analog copy of a digital recording done with mics out in the taper section of the audience. The band set aside part of each venue for tapers to set up their mics and decks, and though I continued to acquire tapes over the next year or so, by Summer 1999 the trading scene had shifted to mp3 and CD copies of digital recordings; there are no analog copies of the band's post–99 shows. The 7/17 tape was a 90-minute Maxell XL-II, the midlevel standard for non-audiophile live-recording traders – I used to buy dozens of them at a go from Terrapin Tapes, a beloved online fan resource now departed.

The 7/17 tape contained six songs, the first four (the night's second set) comprising over an hour of music. I hadn't actually had a chance to listen to the tape prior to that night, but I didn't pay much attention when it came over the bus's speakers; even though I'd excitedly advertised that we were gonna get some West Coast action on the stereo, the crowd was too amped up to stay quiet. I like to imagine that we sang along with the tunes – but then the tape contained *maybe* eight minutes of vocals scattered across seventy minutes of music, so that's not likely.

We got to Limestone late in the morning. I dropped off my backpack and sleeping bag in the kid's tent – was his name Nate? in memory he looks like a Nate, or a Chris – and headed out to find David.

There were roughly 80,000 people gathered at Loring AFB; I found David inside of fifteen minutes. (He had some kind of readily-identifiable flag flying above his trailer.) He worked at the Whitehead Institute, in the mailroom or somesuch; in January we'd had a party at his house, daisy-chaining a half-dozen tape decks to make multiple copies of the 12/30/97 show at Madison Square Garden. He'd lent me a copy of *Live Evil* by Miles Davis, and later that year he'd let me borrow his copies of some Grateful Dead shows from 1974. I didn't understand any of it; I was perfectly happy. I've come to believe the former is prerequisite to the latter, but at the time I figured I just didn't smoke enough weed to know what everyone was talking about. (That's probably true too.)

David's buddies offered me a beer and turned up the stereo, which was playing some live Frank Zappa from back when they were kids. I didn't have a cell phone, had brought only enough money to buy a couple of snacks a day. It hadn't occurred to me that it would be difficult to get food at Loring; like most everyone else I assumed I'd come by it somehow, that the scene would take care of itself somehow. Well, I don't remember starving, and I know David and company had food. I liked not loved the Zappa. I was, as I believe I've mentioned, perfectly happy. It was a little after midday, August 15.

I think it was around 4pm, unironically maybe 4:20, when the first set of the weekend began. I was up near the stage, in front of the keyboardist. Someone around my age in an ostentatious pea-coat told me Paul Desmond's alto sax tone was 'like butter' and I didn't know who he was talking about. That evening I got hit in the face with a glowstick – which is lucky, really, just *one* I mean, considering that at the time several hundred of them, perhaps a thousand, were being whipped through the air by cheering dancing concertgoers. One hit to the face is a small price to pay. I danced and slept in my jeans and smelled like a barnyard animal by the end of the weekend. At 1:30 in the morning on the 16th I lay in the middle of the concert field with the band halfway through an hourlong 'ambient set' – a single free improvisation in a circle of candles dipped over the weekend by fans at a booth onsite – and I figured things couldn't by any reasonable measure be improved upon. I ran into some friends and resented that they were on acid, an attitude I regret no less for better understanding (years after the fact) why I ever held it. I stayed sober and was absolutely certain it was the best concert I'd been to, and many in the crowd seemed to agree.

The festival was called *Lemonwheel*, and over two days the band played ten hours of rock music for one of the biggest concert crowds in the world in 1998. There was a single band on the bill. I'd like to give you an idea: *ten hours* of music, and I paid rapt attention to just about every note of it, dancing my way to exhaustion more than once, certain that I was connecting, connected, part of a larger organism.

On the morning of the 17th I came back to Boston and by the next day, Tuesday, I had more or less physically recovered. I went back to school the next month, nearly failed out of school, got dumped, changed majors, became a familiar sort of college atheist, was consoled in the wake of a suicide and felt like an idiot for it, got dumped, failed to vote in the 2000 election because 'it didn't really matter,' zealously refused any offer of marijuana, and staggered into grad school. In 2000 the band went on hiatus; it regrouped for New Year's Eve 2002, played for another year and a half (during which time I saw five shows, left a tallish brunette with biggish hips for a tallish brunette with biggish hips – going to shows with them both, though not the same show – and [unrelatedly] started spending a good deal of time with the skinny Polish science nerd who's now my wife), and split up 'for good' in 2004.

❤ ☞ ♣ ☞ ✳

lack of understanding is *not* prerequisite to perfect happiness, by the way. i'm so so wrong about so so much and always have been.

❤ ☞ ♣ ☞ ✳

it should've been perfect.

that's the point. it should've been the High Point and Very End. or november 30th should've been, or december 6th. someone should have *stopped* things – or gotten me to stop. you desperately want buffy to come back from the dead so you can have *more fun* but there's also that small matter of needing things to end, not even happily – come on be serious! – but end for realsies, like romance ends, or the right time to joke around, or half-full glasses empty wholly out and time to go on beat it scram. nighttimes into day – or the other way around, probably is what i mean.

or no. no it's the night i wish would stay; which can't.

when my mom died that should've been the end, too. or when i left grad school and became whatever came next. shit that should've been the gauntlet. door closing behind, mind your possessions lest they smash crack in the door and the dust settle upon you and begin, slowly, to turn you to stone. nope though.

you go on living, is the problem. 'how am i supposed to live without you?' well the trick is:

♥ ☞ ✤ ☞ ✻

The crucial fact about traditional dramatic structure is that it's not like life: we don't generally experience 'rising action,' nor do we often go through 'climactic' moments; and 'inciting incidents' tend to be readily identifiable only in retrospect. Never forget that dramatic structure is an lie brilliantly designed to intensify the consciousness-remapping and emotion-hijacking that are the whole point of drama.

Realism and traditional narrative structure are ultimately incompatible: while it's obviously possible to write a 'realist' novel with a big bang at the end, but the closer a representation comes to life, the harder it is to get away with the fundamental *manipulation* of the Big Finish. Any sufficiently detailed rendering of a human life must be anticlimactic or else ring false…unless the storyteller has another out.

Which stories sell?

Courtroom dramas. War stories. Bodice-rippers. Sport. Detective stories. Romantic comedies. Religious stories. Action movies. Horror stories. Fantasy destiny-quests. That sort of thing.

They're all the same story: the story of God arranging events so that the *last* thing to happen is the most important, and reveals the true value of the protagonist. A verdict is rendered. Princes become kings. Friends become lovers. Soldiers are valorous and die. Detectives uncover crimes or epistemologies. Monsters are defeated through pluck, or eat everyone. Vengeance is served cold. One team shows that it deserves to win, and does.

One explanation for literary fiction's loss of visibility and relevance is just this: adults are now able to understand not only that there are no 'happy endings' — now an old idea — but that there are no 'endings,' really. System dynamics mortally wounded fiction long before Youtube came along to befoul its corpse...

♥ ☞ ♣ ☞ ✶

(blah blah blah)

the show on the 7th of december is much loved and you can't blame anyone for that. i think in part because it's so *unserious*. bag > psycho killer to open, seriously? they're just dorking around at that point, and trey manages to screw Psycho Killer up (just like he pissed all over Blister in the Sun in july). it's not like it's a complicated tune, man. it should really read bag > byrne jam > bag > jesus or something; the talking heads tune isn't really the point of the exercise. but it tells you right upfront that the proceedings aren't really to be taken seriously. (phish's version of jesus just left chicago is impressive in its way, but most of the time you almost wouldn't call it 'blues,' where the blues has something to do with emotion and deep cultural roots...)

the show should've ended when the main character ascended to heaven, right? but it goes on, *farcically*. (talking about jesus. ain't we always.) i mean it really is a strong version of JJLC, don't get me wrong, but what's the point? i don't mean for the people there, i mean for *me right now*. viewing the series on dvd as it were. and that's a gorgeous ice > swept > steep > ice four-piece(!!??), but the swept > steep moment is oddly, subtly rushed. they seem to wanna get back to the dorking around. and but me, watching at home on my fully engorged HDTV device with 12-Channel Bigass Sound, well: i wanna replay the scene where they faded Twist down to almost nothing before the segue into Piper, Izabella rocketfall sounds still echoing around the roofbeams, and i was scared exhilarated so full of Moment, darkness flowed past and would give way to day but had not yet been swept away, the danger still lingered, a roar could be heard, i was present at an ending.

man, i wasn't even *at* that show and i still wish we'd all died that night, don't you? don't you want to live forever, or at least a good solid 90 years or something, but don't you *also* want to go at the right moment, trumpets blaring in the background – to see the seals breaking and hear bureaucrat angels barking orders at stubborn mortals failing utterly, even on such a serious occasion, to get their stuff together and get in line? for jesus, i mean. the Revelation. the big finish.

i guess i mean i want the End to matter one way or the other.

❤ ☞ ✤ ☞ ✳

It all comes back to 9/11, right? 'Maybe it was the millennium. No really.' Remember?

The funny thing about Y2K is that it was only the *Christian* millennium in the strictest sense – it wasn't the 2000th year of anyone else's anything, never mind whether you still believe (or ever did) that Jesus of Nazareth was actually born on December 25, Year Zero – but it's also one (peak) moment in a decades-long apocalyptic interval stretching from 1400AH/1979AD on one end, complete with Islamic Revolution in Iran and *my birth yeah yeah!*, and 2012AD (think about it) on the other.[65] Just as many Muslims and Jews have adopted the Gregorian calendar for external timekeeping, keeping 'two sets of books' as it were, the Culture-Wide Bout of 2012-Related Stupidity has seeped into the popular consciousness against every literate person's will. (Even the Mayans didn't think their calendar 'ended' in 2012.)

The attacks of September 2001 were apocalyptic in a specific sense: nearly every single Westerner went to sleep on the 10th in one world and woke on the 11th in another, and the latter had to be encountered *on its own terms,* not those of the old world.[66] Every parameter, from how you defined your politics to what your government was *for,* seemed to change. Even with the anticlimax surrounding the Y2K bug, the attacks still felt, if not right away then shortly after, as the immensity of the change became clear, like the *culmination* of a historical moment. **This bit is handwavey and mawkish, I know, sorry; plus I can't speak for you, duh.** And the coincidence of the Christian millennium, the false security of the late 90s Western economic/speculative boom, the world-historical increase in national and personal interconnectedness (however shallow the new connections might still have been), and the *totality* of media focus on the attacks themselves[67] – to say nothing of, y'know, the startling discovery by a half-billion drowsy nominal grownups that they weren't alone in the world, nor were all brown-skinned folk always in a good mood like their *au pairs* – invested the event with unbearable symbolic weight. Unbearable in the literal sense: look at

---

[65] So do your math: the next round of Islamic millenarianism comes 'round in the 2070s, just in time for 1500AH (if we're still around then). Won't that be nice!

[66] Time to reread our Karl Marx...

[67] (or rather the WTC attack, since apparently there're no human beings in the Pentagon to worry about)

the deformation American society has undergone in the decade since...

Anyhow so for a thousand years you hear blah blah Y2K and then just a nudge past the predicted date, an eyeblink on that timescale, you wake up to hear the TV saying *there is an apocalyptic war going on and has been for decades or centuries, we honestly have no idea, plus in 11 years (just in time for the 15th anniversary of Fall 97, yay!) we're all gonna ascend to New Age Heaven in time for the Age of Aquarius, or else ooze together in a sea of egoless protoplasm beneath the expressionless face of a teenage robot-warrior Pixie Girl if you believe* Neon Genesis Evangelion, *and why wouldn't you?* Well, that kinda news would give pause to the stiffest-spined of mammals, which you and I aren't, no offense.

And that is (or the period is, and continues to be(!!)) the fulcrum; the matrix of transformation. That was the end of one world and the start of something totally new.

but

But it *wasn't* the end. Quite the opposite. There was more to come, most of it terrible, and not just in a Chinese-proverb 'interesting times' sort of way. Just...more. **More life.** More with less, no less! And for those old enough to remember the other time, before the Apocalypse, the hardest thing – if only for a while – would be the superposition of realtime and private time: the 2012 that might've been, say, and the one that merely shittily was. The promised Blessing, continuance and reproduction (remaking) – curdling on the tongue.

...

Disappointing, isn't it? In a way.

Even if Phish *are* playing better now than ever.

❤ ☞ ✤ ☞ ✽

If I seem to be belaboring a simple point – things change, but nothing really ends – which, among others, *Watchmen* made in a single panel 25 years ago, I'm sorry; and I'm sorry there isn't more Phish in the preceding few pages. Really I am. As it happens, I interrupted writing the 12/6 entry to put this together. It's the first time I've done that in the process of writing this book. Nested feelings.

I don't think I can write about the rest of the month, is the thing. Not as I've written about the first of it.

Formally there's little I can say about the last five shows of the tour without repeating myself more than I already have. The transition from pinpoint machine-funk to pure aural sculpture (with attendant loss of specificity, even precision) is well underway at this point, and what will become known to some fans as the band's 'millennial' sound is present in embryonic form: having taken a sedimentary approach in the 11/23 Gin and 11/26 Zero, layering Hendrix-inspired guitar cloudwork and atmospheric keyboards atop a slowly-shifting bass/drums roil, the band spent much of the second Albany set working in their so-fast-it's-slow-again register, applying the catastrophic sonics of Saw It Again to hyperactive cut-time beats in a long Piper and unhinged Caspian > Izabella. (The show's even got a Zero to close the first set – talk about repeating yourself!). The Albany Ghost and Hood are experiments in the same vein – the former a Gin-soaked Biggest Smile competition, the latter a daring rhythmic-ambient exploration. Rochester's big jams self-immolate or just expire right onstage, in a foreshadowing of the terminally druggy 1999–2000 sound. The churchly Simple from Penn State showcases the band's deepening engagement with sonic textures, revealing over 30 blissful minutes a safe path from that song's gentle I-IV-V outro stroll to an anthemic passage reminiscent of Simple itself, and then out into the world again via a sublime ten-minute dissolution (and frightening Bowie tease) that recalls the 12/6 Twist.

To be sure, there's plenty of magic in those last five shows, and if you enjoy Phish's (kind of) music at all then I recommend them to you without reservation – all except maybe the 12/11 Rochester show, which might not be the worst show of the month but is probably the most *boring*. (So I guess it's the worst. How else would you measure?) The Penn State show's got that heartbreaking Stash > Hydrogen pairing, after all, with the latter tune played less sleepily than in Hampton but still shot through with powerful emotion. (Shame about the full-band fuckup at the start of Weekapaug…) And yeah, the 12/7 show is a nonstop party, a throwback to the olden days in its Sure Yeah Why Not YEAH! setlist and goofball energy, not to mention the outlandish Tube jam, wonderfully patient Timber, and pleasantly dreadful Boogie On. It's almost all well played and suffused with an admirable generosity of spirit.

But I hear these shows as echoes of the *buildup* and *culmination* which the first three weeks of tour inescapably are to me. Yes, yes: the improvisation in the first Albany show is as demonically aggressive as the blowout in Winston-Salem, the Ya Mar and Theme and Ghost from the next night have the groove and grandeur and loping effortlessness of the Philly shows, and even the listless and repetitive Rochester Ghost is partly redeemed by a manic reprise of that evening's hypoxic first-set Disease. But so what? The music might be great, the experience was probably absolute bliss for those lucky enough to attend (and is complicated bliss for me now, or at minimum pleasurably complicated) (I mean think of the 'bring in the Dude' joy/stupidity from the final night in Albany!) (but it just *suuuucks* on tape), but if this is a story then we're well into the 'fifth separate moment where the movie of *Return of the King* could have ended, making everyone but the Tolkien purists happy' part of the story – excuse me, the Story, can't forget my portentous-capitalization habit this close to the end...

Nothing could be tackier than invoking 9/11 in a book about Phish tour, *nothing*. I get that. But the actual tour's actual tagline actually was **PHISH DESTROYS AMERICA**. C'mon. C'mon! You think I pulled 'apocalyptic time' purely out of my solipsism-thought-ass?

The music is the music and I hope you can come to it on its own terms, as I've tried and failed to do; but hopefully the nature of that failure holds interest for you, as it does for me (and mental health professionals everywhere). That narrativizing impulse, the craving for apocalypse, has always been a big part of my deep love and sometimes angry or incoherent relationship for this band and their music. And part of the reason I've been tearing my hair out for many a thousand words here is that my two warring impulses – to come to the music empty, and to add the music as one more layer of the inner noise that I've believed for so foolishly long is **who I really am** – give me incomparable but equally uplifting experiences of *bliss*. Of simplicity or multiplicity; of emptiness and business; of total surrender to the moment, and then the bliss of gathering every past movement and dwelling into one supra-experience – feel free to reread that RAW quote about 'reality tunnels' and 'lyrical Utopianism' now.

So as much as I'd like to write 200 pages of 'criticism' of/about these shows, or even just these recordings, you and I musta known we couldn't go that long without a change of vibe – at some point we've gotta face the fact that since we're (right?) not God, our experience and re-presentation of this music's gotta be imperfect, and those imperfections will multiply and deepen, premature behavioural optimizations and cognitive shortcuts will start to tell, to overtake the 'objective' attempt or just shatter the pretense thereof...we're where we must've figured on being, talking about what we talk about when we talk about Phish. I've been obsessed with this band for a lot of my life but my obsession isn't ultimately about them; they're just a guitar/piano rock band and anyway they couldn't shine John Coltrane's shoes.[68]

I wanna say we're talking about the bliss we find in the music, what we so desperately want and even need; but sometimes I think it's just wanting we're talking about. Wanting together. Straining to escape different somethings via shared means.

i *don't* want to know i'll die. i hate it. the sound that i am. everything i know i know in my own voice and i know i'll die. more life? no, no more. never never never. not afterward.

but there's another knowing past that. true music is an invitation to know that it makes no difference. can't take anything from you.

---

[68] I kid. But still, if at the Pearly Gates you're given the choice, for your eternal soundtrack, between *A Love Supreme* and almost any other music mentioned here, you better choose Trane and say hi for me.

He slew them, at surprising distances, with his gun.
Over a body held in his hand, his head was bowed low,
But not in grief.

He put them where they are, and there we see them:
In our imagination.

What is love?

One name for it is knowledge.
   —Robert Penn Warren

we deflate

ACKNOWLEDGEMENTS

To my wife and son: thank you so much for all you do and have done, for not holding against me the hours I stole (during naps, workdays, weekends, evenings) in order to finish this work. Fortunately, life without you is impossible: 'fortunately' because it's also undesirable. I love you both.

Many thanks also to the folks who've shared my obsession over the years – dear friends like Laurie and Goliath's Daddy, classy chatterers and familiar (virtual) faces like andrewrose, benhatley, n00b100, conradjohansen, dirk420, bertoletdown, kevin are hollo, benjy eisen, MrCompletely, Rosemary of Digest fame, david r., the dude at Lemonwheel with the tent, and so damned many others. And thanks too to 'Mr Miner,' David Calarco, whose site was a big part of what brought me back to the fandom a few years ago, and a great help to me as I reencountered the band's history.

Thanks to Mary, Sinclair, and the other enablers at Cafe Luna.

APOLOGIES AND RECOMMENDATIONS

Are you relatively new to Phish, and skipping around the book looking for a foothold? Consider listening to 15 August 2011,

17 November 1997, and/or New Year's Eve 1995 – all of which are available as affordable high-quality professional soundboard recordings. The Denver show (11/17/97, discussed earlier) will give you a sense of the sounds and shapes I've been talking about; NYE 95 is a three-set distillation of Phish's career pre–1997; 8/15/11 is a perfect introduction to the band's work since reforming in 2009.

Nearly every live Phish show is listed, with links to v0 mp3 files, in an invaluable single file online – google *hoydog23 spreadsheet* for the Thing Itself.

The studio albums *Billy Breathes* and *Rift* nicely capture the band's rustic-Americana and virtuosic prog-rock sides, and are their most coherent studio efforts. Though only *Billy* has the critics on its side, *Rift* contains the band's strongest batch of early songs – with a workable album concept to boot.

If you're curious about how Phish fans talk to each other, try the *phish.net* forum.

END OF SESSION

I had intended for this book to mark the end of my involvement with Phish fandom. As I finish this draft, I'm no longer sure. It's fun talking about this stuff, and fun is alright.

But I'd like to take a break at the very least. The original notion was '1997+15 & 1999+15,' which should make clear what I'd hoped to do next in this vein, but as I found myself saying a few pages ago, Fall 97 is unquestionably the center of gravity of my fandom: the core of an obsession which, through ebb and flow and transformation, has been central to my identity for half my life. I've had my say on that subject. Enough.

Please drop a line and let me know what you thought of the book – most places online I go by **waxbanks**.

Thank you so much for sharing this music with me.

WALLY HOLLAND
CAMBRIDGE MA
OCTOBER 2012

Walter Holland was born in San Juan, grew up near Houston and then near Buffalo, and now lives in Cambridge. He has written several other books (available wherever you got this one), including *The Allworlds Catalogue*; *Falsehoods, Concerns*; and *Fixing You*.

Walter can be found online at *blog.waxbanks.net*.

Made in the USA
Lexington, KY
01 August 2014